THE SENIOR DRIVER'S SURVIVAL GUIDE

WHAT OLDER DRIVERS MUST KNOW TO PROTECT THEIR DRIVING PRIVILEGES IN THEIR GOLDEN YEARS

NORMAN KLEIN

authorHOUSE®

AuthorHouse™
1663 Liberty Drive
Bloomington, IN 47403
www.authorhouse.com
Phone: 1-800-839-8640

First published by AuthorHouse 3/19/2010

ISBN: 978-1-4520-0786-1 (e)
ISBN: 978-1-4490-6855-4 (sc)

Printed in the United States of America
Bloomington, Indiana

This book is printed on acid-free paper.

ALSO BY NORMAN KLEIN

"Drive Without Fear"

The Insecure Driver's Guide
To Independence And
Anxiety-Free Driving

Acknowledgments

I wish to thank my two sons, Doctor Howard and Attorney David, for their assistance and encouragement. Thanks to my wife, Marylin, for her grammatical help. I would also like to thank Anne McCaul for the great job she did preparing my manuscript for publication. Last, but not least, I have to give credit to the thousands of seniors I taught who gave me the knowledge which enabled me to write this book.

For my two super sons, Howard and David. Also for my brother, Milton, and in memory of brother, Ben, sisters, Ethel Rose, Jean, and Mary, and my irreplaceable friend, Maishie.

ABOUT THE BOOK

Norman Klein has devoted thirty-six years to finding ways to help the elderly drive safely. There is no doubt that a crisis is looming for senior drivers. The number of drivers over sixty-five is increasing three times as much as all other age groups. Within the next twenty years, millions of drivers over eighty years of age will be out on the road.

If senior drivers continue to commit accidents because of inattention or lack of concentration, many states will insist upon re-examinations.

Reading this book and heeding its contents will surely help to remedy this serious problem for drivers in their "golden" years.

His previous book *"Drive Without Fear,"* has been acclaimed by those who read the book. Thousands of readers have conquered their fear and are now driving safely.

"The Senior Driver's Survival Guide" is an important book which has the power to save lives. The knowledge it contains will enable seniors to drive safely and protect their driving privileges.

Foreword

The author has gathered the information and recommendations in this book after many years in the driver-training field and much of it is based on his opinions and observations. Therefore, it should not be construed as being absolutely correct and no guarantee is made that all safety measures have been met and included. The purpose of this book is to refresh, advise and re-educate senior drivers, especially those in their eighties and nineties.

INTRODUCTION

As people are living longer, the number of older drivers on the road is increasing rapidly. According to Government statistics, the number of drivers over sixty-five is multiplying three times as much as other age groups. These numbers will continue to proliferate until millions will be driving in their eighties and nineties.

Older folks take more medication and are susceptible to Alzheimer's and Parkinson's disease as well as dementia and failing vision, among other ailments. They have shorter attention spans and do not process information as they did when they were younger.

Driving an automobile is without question a vital part of a senior's self-esteem, happiness and independence. Except for losing a loved one, surrendering a drivers' license can be the most traumatic and devastating blow a senior may encounter. Many seniors find themselves in this heart-wrenching situation that destroys their freedom.

Over the years, driving a motor vehicle has become increasingly hazardous. Drive in any city or populous area and it would be unusual if you did not witness driving infractions. Driving over the speed limit is a common practice as is going through traffic lights when they change to red.

When seniors commit traffic violations they are held more accountable because of their age. It is probable that older drivers will be confronted with a crisis which could jeopardize their driving future. If their driving record falls below that of the general public it is likely that they will be asked to take a re-examination. Some of them will lack the confidence to be re-examined and will forfeit their licenses.

After years of teaching older drivers, I have realized that except for debilitating illnesses, lack of concentration was the overwhelming reason for their driving mishaps. Seniors must do their utmost to avoid accidents which reflect lack of concentration. They must make every effort to stay focused and abstain from getting distracted. It is my wish that seniors reading this book will be better prepared to maintain their driving privileges.

Table of Contents

INTRODUCTION xv
PREFACE xxi

CHAPTER 1 STAYING FOCUSED . . . . ¯ . . 1
    Hand-Over-Hand Turning 6
    Steering - The Key to Driving 8
    Incorrect Turning. 8
    Rules to Remember 8

CHAPTER 2 HOW TO COPE WITH TRACTOR-
    TRAILERS AND ANTI-LOCK BRAKES 11
    Blind Spots 13
    "Pay Attention to Trucks' Turn Signals" 14
    Truck Drivers with Little Sleep Perform Poorly Study Shows
    18
    Anti-Lock Brakes ("ABS") 19
    Hold it down and do not pump the brake. 22
    Pedestrians vs. Drivers 22
    Position of "No Turn on Red" Signs 23
    Posted Speed Limits. 24

CHAPTER 3 LEFT TURNS. 25
    Turning Left on Red 26
    The Red Light Dilemma 27
    Left Turns, Green Arrows and Green Lights. 28
    Yield To Motorcycles 29
    Watching A Left Turn Accident Unfold 30
    A Left Turn Malaise. 31
    Do Not Get Moving Violations. 32
    Important Rules for Seniors and Others. 33
    Two-Way Stop Signs 36
    Four-Way Stop Signs 36

Passing a Public Bus. 37

CHAPTER 4 WOMEN DRIVERS. 38
Women and Predators 44

CHAPTER 5 MALE DRIVERS 47
Los Angeles Drivers 50
Other Tips. 52
Men Afraid to Drive 54

CHAPTER 6 TIPS FOR THE ELDERLY 55
School Buses 55
Letting Cars Out of Driveways 56
Letting Pedestrians Walk in Front of You 57
Vision Problems. 57
Emergency Vehicles 58
Do Not Overreact 59
Watch For Pedestrians 59
Sport Utility Vehicles. 60
The Following Statements are True or False 61
Answers to True or False 62
Railroad Crossings. 63
Braking Not Always Best 63
Brake Failure 64
Stalling 64
Headlight Failure. 65
Facing a Rise in Hit-And-Run Accidents 65
The Meaning of Yellow Lines. 67
The Meaning of White Lines 68

CHAPTER 7 ACCIDENT-FREE DRIVING 69
Stay In Your Lane 69
Check Traffic Before Changing Lanes 69
Do Not Stare at Distractions 71
You Could Steer Incorrectly or Brake at the Wrong Time
and Cause an Accident. 72
Anticipate Problems. 72

Driving in Snow, Rain and at Night. 73
Rear-End Collisions. 76
Driving in the Rain 77
Space Cushion 78
Reaction Time 78
Night Driving 79
Drive Right at Night 79
Driving Tips 79
Hidden Stop Sign 80
Don't be a Horn Blower. 81
Potholes. 81
If Key is Stuck and Wheel is Locked 82
Flashing Lights 82
The Driver Behind You 83
Decisions. 84

CHAPTER 8 WHEN TO GIVE UP DRIVING 85
Problems Dealing With Seniors. 91
Dementia. 92

CHAPTER 9 REVERSE - SHOPPING CENTER -
LIMITED ACCESS HIGHWAYS - FREEWAYS 94
Backing Out of Parking Spaces 95
Parking in Shopping Centers 95
Driving in Shopping Centers. 96
Entering a Freeway or Limited Access Highway. 97

CHAPTER 10 USING YOUR VISION CORRECTLY . 100
Questions and Answers 100
Follow the Dark Streak 100
Turned Around Stop Signs. 107
Bicycle Riders 107
The Most Irritating Infractions of Drivers 108

CHAPTER 11 VITAL RULES FOR SENIORS AND
EVERYONE ELSE. 110
Changing Lights 114

CHAPTER 12 THE DRIVING TEST 116
    Be Prepared 120

CHAPTER 13 WHAT GRANDPARENTS SHOULD
    KNOW 121
    Taking Care of Your Vehicle 123
    Fluids to Watch 123
    Donating Your Car 125
    How Grandparents Help 125
    Cell Phones 126
    Senior Pedestrians 127
    A Preventable Accident 128
    Driving a Stick Shift 130

CHAPTER 14 CONCLUSION 131
    Road Rage 132
    Drunk Drivers 133
    Look Ahead 135

PREFACE

Senior Drivers! Your future is in jeopardy.   A very disturbing situation is developing in the United States. As people are living longer more of the elderly will be driving as never before.

I was in the driver training field for thirty-six years and personally taught thousands of people, including many seniors.

In October 1989, the *Philadelphia Inquirer* featured me in a special section about the driving problems of older people. Teaching many of them familiarized me with their shortcomings.

The proliferation of older drivers on the roadways will undoubtedly create hazards unless they take it upon themselves to concentrate and focus on their driving and not be distracted. They must be made aware of their inclination to daydream which is prevalent in many of them, especially those in their eighties and older.

Driving slowing in traffic is not the answer. This could cause accidents. Driving too fast would be worse since an octogenarian's attention span and concentration would be questionable. It does not matter how skillful you once were. Aging diminishes our skills in almost all areas, including driving a motor vehicle. Driving today has become more complex as many more cars are on the road. When seniors started to drive, turnpikes and expressways were non-existent.

It is for these reasons that I decided to write "The Senior Driver's Survival Guide," which alerts the older driver to the crucial significance of complete concentration when behind the wheel.

A few years ago, I wrote *"Drive Without Fear"* for people afraid to drive. The success of the book has been substantiated by the 15 5 star reviews [unsolicited] which can be seen on the *Amazon. com* website. No doubt, the number of five star reviews will continue to increase. These reviews are from diverse parts of the Country. Among them are Texas, Minnesota, Maine, California and Maryland.

The book has been acclaimed by its readers who credit me with allaying their fear of driving. I believe that you will be impressed if you go to *Amazon.com*'s website and read the reviews.

After observing the type of accidents seniors were having and realizing how their ranks were exploding, I decided to write *"The Senior Drivers Survival Guide" - "What You Must Know To Protect Your Driving Privilege."*

Its contents can enable them to drive with a more acute awareness and help them to be better drivers in their "golden" years.

CHAPTER 1
STAYING FOCUSED

You are driving on a well-traveled street in your city. You are a retired senior citizen and have been driving for fifty-five years. The street has traffic lights at almost every intersection and the traffic is flowing smoothly.

You turn on the radio to listen to your favorite sports station. Because the traffic is moving smoothly, you don't watch the road for a few seconds. You look ahead at the street and to your astonishment you see the traffic in front of you has stopped. You hit the brake and luckily you stop in time, but the next time this happens you might not be so fortunate. What you should have known was that traffic can change in a few seconds.

You realize that to let your attention wander aimlessly is too hazardous. Rear-end collisions happen everywhere, everyday and the reasons (except for speeding) are almost always the same - inattention, distractions and allowing your mind to wander.

Not focusing on your driving is the central theme of this book and it will be repeated constantly. It does not matter how skillful you are or were. If you do not concentrate one hundred percent of the time, you are placing yourself and others in jeopardy.

An amusing article in the *Philadelphia Inquirer* (January 2000) related how an Assemblyman on his way to testify about distracted drivers was rear-ended by an older driver. The driver who hit his car was reaching for popcorn while taking his eyes away from the road.

New York and New Jersey have laws where it is illegal to hold a cell phone while driving. This law makes using a hand-held phone a secondary offense. This means that you cannot be pulled over and ticketed unless you have committed another illegal offense.

It is imperative for senior drivers not to use cell phones or hands-free phones while driving. As the years go by it takes a greater effort to concentrate. Senior drivers do not need cell phones to add to this inclination towards distractions.

Except for failing health, vision and poor driving skills, lack of concentration is the single greatest cause of accidents caused by older drivers.

Drivers (usually over seventy) have a proclivity towards daydreaming while behind the wheel. This happens usually when they are alone in the car. Consequently, while daydreaming they may not be able to recognize slowing or stopped traffic. Unfortunately, they are abruptly brought to their senses by causing a rear-end collision.

A friend of mine who fits into this category had four accidents in the space of eighteen months. He came to me for advice after his lady friend told me her children had advised her not to accompany him while he was driving. She informed me that while he was driving he was not attentive to traffic in front of him, especially when he insisted on talking.

He came to me for a test drive. I noticed that when he spoke to me he had a tendency to drive at his own speed. At times he would fall behind traffic, thus becoming a traffic hazard. To sum up his driving habits, I informed him that all his driving problems were caused by a lack of total concentration. Many people are not capable of driving attentively and carrying on a conversation at the same time.

My friend was basically a capable driver with good motor skills. Upon questioning him, I discovered that while driving, he looked at every billboard he passed and frequently paid too much attention to women walking on the sidewalk. To put it succinctly, he was guilty of doing what many other senior drivers do. After driving for fifty years, people tend to become careless and do not concentrate, become easily distracted, daydream and become a hazard on the road.

My friend accepted my evaluation insomuch as his lady friend had threatened to leave him if he didn't change his driving habits. Recently he drove to Florida from Philadelphia to visit her without any driving mishaps. He knows now the importance of staying focused and his lady friend is not afraid to ride with him in the driver's seat.

There are other precautions seniors should take but far and away no rule is as important as focusing completely on their driving. Total concentration is of paramount importance for senior citizens.

Aging doesn't only affect one's driving ability. The world's best athletes undergo changes as they age. The skills of most athletes diminish after the age of thirty. There are some exceptions for different sports. A golfer can compete into his or her middle ages. Some baseball pitchers extend their careers up to the age of forty. In basketball, age is a dominant factor because speed is essential. After the age of thirty, most of them reach their prime and then regress. Football players do not last too long since strength, speed and agility are necessary to their success. The average football player's career is usually shorter than in other sports.

In every sport concentration is important for success and any athlete who does not concentrate will not be successful. If an athlete doesn't stay focused and commits an error he may be taken out of the game. The opposing team may score.

However, when a person driving a vehicle has an accident by not concentrating property is damaged and fatalities may occur.

If an older driver has an accident and is found to be at fault that person will almost certainly be required to take a re-examination. A seventy-year old woman in my neighborhood was told to take a re-examination because she drove the wrong way on a one-way street. She decided to surrender her driving license because of her fear of a re-examination.

Because of their age, seniors' insurance premiums are usually higher. If involved in an accident, the premiums could rise drastically. Therefore, it is important for seniors to be alert and focused one hundred percent of the time. The privilege of driving and being independent is too important to do otherwise.

If seniors continue to have accidents caused by inattentiveness, the public will clamor for re-examinations, something that seniors oppose and fear.

Rear-end collisions are the most prevalent of all vehicle accidents and lack of concentration is the leading cause. Older drivers are more prone to having this type of accident because of their tendency to daydream while behind the wheel.

The records show that when older people are injured in an auto accident, they do not heal as well as younger people. The effects of their injuries could stay with them for the rest of their lives.

This is reason enough for older drivers to examine their driving habits and try their best to avoid accidents. This is no easy task.

Driving an automobile involves factors such as reaction time, depth perception, vision, *etc.* As people get older their driving skills diminish. Therefore, it is imperative that they stay alert and only concentrate on their driving when behind the wheel.

I know this sounds like a broken record, but without total concentration older drivers will not retain their privilege to drive.

Too many drivers and passengers do not wear seatbelts. In severe accidents, the people killed are usually ejected from the car because they were not wearing a seatbelt.

Always wear your seatbelt. Keep the lap belt below your abdomen and not above your hips. If you are stopped by an officer for another violation, you will get a separate citation for not wearing your seatbelt.

Many people turn the wheel with the push-pull method. The wheel is held at four o'clock with the right hand and eight o'clock with the left hand. For right turns, you move the left hand towards twelve o'clock and follow with the right hand pushing the steering wheel in the same direction. For left turns you start with the right hand. If you are not turning hand-over-hand, you are probably turning push-pull. If you are turning casually, push-pull is okay. If you have an older car, you may be more inclined to use hand-over-hand since older cars were built with larger steering wheels. If you have short arms, hand-over-hand turning may be too difficult. When you have to turn quickly from one direction to another, hand -over-hand would be best. In some states the driving test includes a serpentine course and you would not be able to do it satisfactorily if you did it push-pull. A seventy-year old former student of mine was called in to take a re-exam. He flunked the test because he didn't turn hand-over-hand and could not stay in the lane. I taught him how to steer hand-over-hand and he regained his license.

Hand-Over-Hand Turning

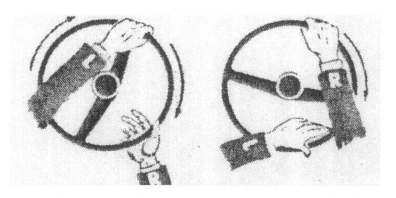

As your left hand begins to turn, you must release the wheel with your right hand. The right hand then grasps the steering wheel near the top of the wheel as the left hand is released from the wheel and continues to turn the wheel. This process is repeated as many times as necessary to change the direction of the vehicle to the new heading. The average right turn should take three turns, left, right and left. For the left turn it would be right, left, right. As your right hand turns, you should release the wheel with your left hand and vice-versa. If you have been driving all these years without hand-over-hand turning, try to adjust. Someday you may be asked to take a re-examination, so get it right now. Practice on an empty parking lot at first.

Steering - The Key to Driving

Steering is the key to driving. In my experience, people who could not learn to steer could not learn to drive. Fortunately, the number of people who can't steer well enough to drive is small.

Incorrect Turning

There are probably many older drivers who have been turning the wheel incorrectly all of their lives. They were either self-taught or taught incorrectly by a friend or relative. Instead of turning hand-over-hand, they turn the wheel with both hands with short jerky movements. At the end of each turn, the wheel is released and then turned again.

If you have an older car, you may be inclined to turn this way as these cars have larger wheels. If you are short with small arms (especially women), hand-over-hand turning may be more difficult. For casual turning when not in a hurry, hand-over-hand is not a necessity. Do not turn hand-over-hand on a road with gradual curves, but on a sharper or more pronounced curve use hand-over-hand. As you become more comfortable with both turning methods, you will automatically use the correct method without thinking.

Rules to Remember

1. Never watch the nose of the car.
2. Look straight ahead into the center of your driving path.
3. Guide your body or your nose, not the car.
4. At speeds of twenty-five or thirty, look ahead about five hundred feet (city block).

5. Always turn off the ignition when getting fuel for your car and be sure no one is lighting or smoking a cigarette near your car while the gasoline is flowing into the gas tank.

6. Never pick up hitchhikers.

7. Head restraints should be raised level with your ears.

8. If your car is being bumped intentionally, do not stop. Drive to a police station, convenience store, or gas station and report it.

9. Drive as though your life depends on it because it does.

10. Always inspect the tires before you drive.

11. Icy roads are most hazardous when the temperature is thirty-two degrees. Never use cruise control on icy roads.

Although older motorists are guiltier of daydreaming when driving, concentration is just as important for all drivers. I was once driving in stalled traffic during the Christmas season when a young male driver struck me from behind. Without thinking clearly and obviously in a hurry, he swung out of his lane and crashed into the back of my car. Luckily I was wearing a seatbelt or I would have been thrown against the windshield. I suffered a severe whiplash injury and had to wear a neck brace for a long time.

Concentration is important in any endeavor, but as it applies to driving an automobile, lack of it is deadly. If you do not concentrate when you engage in sports, you may cost your team a victory or be injured. An accident caused by inattention with serious damage to people or property is irreversible. Mistakes made while you are doing your income taxes can be corrected but a human life cannot be replaced.

The introduction of the automobile into the world brought huge advances in industry, transportation and a way of life for all. However, with it came an unparalleled number of fatalities, injuries, and damage to property. Unfortunately, the passage of time has not alleviated this critical situation because of the human element. It seems that people's natural characteristics do not and will not change and lives will continue to be lost on our nation's roads and highways.

"I have great extra-sensory perception for this sort of thing."

CHAPTER 2
How to Cope with Tractor-Trailers and Anti-Lock Brakes

Driving tractor-trailers (rigs), tankers and flatbeds is considered to be among the most dangerous occupations in the country. Approximately six-hundred drivers a year die in rollover or jack-knifing accidents.

Large rigs can roll over when going too fast on curves or when making lane changes too quickly. It is also possible for rigs to roll over by hitting a curb while cornering. Truck accidents due to jack- knifing can occur when the drive wheels are locked and they come into contact with a slick spot. An empty tanker or rig is more than twice as likely to jack-knife than a fully loaded one. Jack-knifing will most likely cause a rollover. A truck driver can best avoid jack- knifing by prudent braking. However, jack-knifing can happen when the driver tries to avoid an accident by braking suddenly. Sometimes the truck driver may be sleep-deprived and cannot see a traffic problem in front of him quickly enough.

Although trucker drivers are almost always blamed for accidents it is not always their fault. Errant drivers do not realize the skill and knowledge required to maneuver a rig, tanker or flatbed. These drivers thoughtlessly cut in front of rigs forcing the truck driver to brake too hard. They may not realize that these larger vehicles cannot change direction as easily as the average sized vehicle.

There are other precautions a driver can take to avoid accidents with tractor-trailers. Never make a left turn in front of an oncoming truck.

Do not change lanes abruptly in front of trucks especially tractor-trailers. Do not do anything to cause a truck driver to brake quickly. Do not merge improperly in traffic when a truck is involved. Don't drive between trucks. Do not pull out onto the road in front of trucks. The whole point is to not cause a truck driver to slow down abruptly.

A perfect example of a tragic accident occurred in Pennsylvania by a thoughtless driver who swerved in front of a truck to help someone on the shoulder of the road.

The truck driver was forced to stop suddenly. Consequently, the driver behind the truck slammed into the rear of the tractor-trailer and was also struck from behind by a second car. The driver of the first vehicle behind the truck was killed and two women in the second car were injured.

Accidents of this type are frequent because too many drivers do not realize tractor-trailers, flatbeds and rigs cannot stop or maneuver as easily as passenger vehicles.

People driving on the highways are being killed or maimed needlessly by truck drivers who are operating their vehicles in an unsafe manner. Thousands of truck drivers obtained their licenses illegally because of fraudulent practices. Many of them are immigrants who can barely read. The need for truck drivers has exploded twenty-five times in the last twenty five years. As a result, the trucking firms do not investigate the history of the applicant as they should.

All senior drivers should be aware of the many hazards involving trucks as should all drivers. Stay away from trucks as much as possible.

Blind Spots

Many automobile drivers are unaware that trucks and buses have three blind spots behind them. One blind spot is when you are in the left lane next to the truck or bus. The driver may not see you if you are too close to the left side of his vehicle.

Another blind spot occurs when an automobile stays too close on the right side of the truck or bus. A car in this position is probably less visible to the commercial driver than a car on the left side. The driver of the automobile should stay as close as possible to the right edge of the lane and move away as soon as possible.

The third blind spot is directly behind the truck or bus. Automobile drivers should not stay too close to the rear of the truck or bus since they are not visible to the commercial driver. They also cannot observe the traffic scene ahead.

Tractor-trailers and large trucks pose a greater hazard at night than during the day. The taillights on most tractor-trailers are smaller than those on many passenger cars. Therefore, passenger car drivers have to be especially careful on dimly lit roads. It is mandatory for trucks to have bars in the rear to prevent "under ride" collisions. However, many trucks and tractor-trailers do not have sidebars or sidelights making it very hazardous for drivers when the trucks are backing out onto a dark road.

When driving in a city or a town do not stay on the right side of a large truck. When a truck driver has to make a right turn he swings to the left. He may not see you on his right side. Many a car driver has been jammed between a truck and the curb.

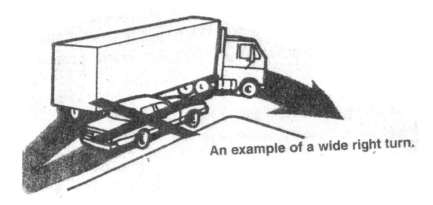

An example of a wide right turn.

"Pay Attention to Trucks' Turn Signals"

Near Philadelphia, on May 25, 1995 at 6:30 A.M., a tanker truck carrying liquid carbon dioxide overturned at the juncture of the Blue Route (Interstate 476) and the Schuylkill Expressway (Interstate 76) in Pennsylvania.

Approximately 83,000 vehicles came to a standstill for five hours. People couldn't get to work, some missed important business meetings, sick people missed doctor's appointments, school buses were filled with restless children, and others missed their flights at the airport.

Many motorists not familiar with the area were forced to leave the highway and blunder onto secondary streets to get to their destinations. People had to be evacuated from their homes since liquid carbon dioxide comes under the Hazardous Material Act.

It boggles my mind to realize that this chaotic scene was caused by one truck driver who disrupted the lives of at least 100,000 people. State Police said the accident occurred when the truck overshot the exit and attempted to turn from a middle lane instead of the right lane. Eyewitnesses stated that the truck appeared to be moving too fast and flipped over onto its side. The driver was pinned against the dashboard and had to be cut out of the cab. A helicopter rushed the injured truck driver to a hospital where he was reported to be in serious condition.

In this particular accident, the truck driver was injured. However, every year approximately 4,500 to 5,000 people are killed in truck accidents. Most of these truck crashes are avoidable. The person responsible in most cases seems to be the truck driver.

In April 1995, NBC television exposed some of the unsafe practices of truck drivers. A truck driver was monitored during a cross country run. He drove twenty hours without sleep. He slept twenty-one hours in six days. By law, a truck driver is supposed to rest eight hours after driving for ten hours.

There are check points along the highway where the truck driver is stopped for examination of his log book. The trucker may enter false figures in his log book and he continues on his way. The authorities at the check points know that his log books are doctored, but nothing is done about it. The truckers say that to earn enough money they must keep moving. NBC stated that truck drivers admit that they doctor their log books.

The particular driver who was monitored for the NBC program was fired by the company for using amphetamines. It didn't take him long to be hired by another trucking company.

NBC also reported a horrifying crash when a tractor trailer hit a vehicle with four young people inside. The truck driver fell asleep and killed the occupants of the car. The truck driver received four months in jail for snuffing out the lives of those young people. This type of accident is not an isolated case.

At times, traffic slows down and for various reasons the truck driver is not aware of the potential danger. He may be tired, not alert, sleepy or not focused. He can't or doesn't slow down in time and human lives are needlessly lost. It is also not uncommon for tractor trailers to overturn or crash into guard rails critically injuring the driver and maiming or killing innocent people. The reasons are almost always the same, excessive speed on curves, driving without enough sleep or not allowing enough space between his truck and car in front of him.

On January 22, 1996, the manager of a cable company in Lancaster was killed when his sport-utility vehicle was crushed between two tractor-trailers on a foggy section of Route 30 in Chester County, Pennsylvania. He was stopped behind one rig at a red light when the second tractor-trailer rammed him from behind. This tragedy typifies the havoc that is perpetrated on innocent people.

A massive tractor-trailer roaring down the highway at seventy or seventy-five miles an hour is not easy to slow down or stop. People who frequently use limited access highways know the fear of being tailgated by a huge tractor-trailer or large truck. They show no mercy. Anyone in this predicament has to go faster in order to move into another lane. To do this, you have to be an experienced driver. This situation is not for the faint-hearted or novice.

When I drive on a highway, I try to stay five or six car lengths away from the vehicle in front of me, or one car length for every ten miles an hour. Recently on I-95 in Pennsylvania a huge tractor-trailer loomed behind me. I pressed down on the accelerator to get away, but as I drove faster the truck driver kept closing in on me. It seemed as if the truck was three feet behind me. If I wanted to slow down for any reason there was a good chance I would be mashed.

It is idiotic for a truck driver to tailgate, especially at high speeds, but many truck drivers bully automobile drivers into submission. I have seen tractors hauling a double trailer racing at speeds over seventy miles an hour. Tractors hauling two trailers should be outlawed. The behemoths on the road are the most dangerous since they would be the most difficult to slow down or stop in an emergency. It is obvious that the trucking industry places financial gain above human lives.

It is noteworthy that bus drivers are not involved in fatal crashes nearly as much as truck drivers. The reason seems to be obvious. Apparently, bus drivers get enough sleep and operate on a set schedule. They also do not jackknife as they usually are not attached to another carrier.

The best way to avoid a collision with a truck is to stay away from it as much as possible. When you are passing a truck or bus be sure to accelerate so you can move quickly away from the blind spot. Do not slow down. Remember that a tractor-trailer going at a high speed may not be able to slow down enough to reduce his braking distance. After passing, never pull back in front until you can see the truck or bus in your rear view mirror. As soon as you can, move into another lane.

Truck Drivers with Little Sleep Perform Poorly Study Shows

Tired truck drivers are dangerous not only to themselves but to others on the road.

A new study by the University of Pennsylvania School of Medicine found that long-distance drivers who slept less than five hours a night had poor reaction times and steering ability.

Surveying more than 1,300 truck drivers, the researchers found that about 13 percent reported getting only five hours of shut-eye a night on a regular basis.

Researchers then gave 406 of the drivers tests that analyzed attention and reaction time and "lane tracking ability." Drivers who got eight hours of sleep did relatively well on the tests, with about 10 percent failing two of three of the tests. Of those who got five hours of sleep, about half did not do well.

Many truck accidents are also caused by mechanical failure. In some instances, it is has been proven that the owners of the truck company knew about the truck's shortcomings but they allowed the trucks to operate to save the cost of repair. When this happens, the company is sued and deservedly so. Human lives should not be sacrificed because of greed.

Since most highways do not provide separate lanes for trucks, accidents with other vehicles are inevitable. The present apathy toward truck-related fatalities must be addressed. Unfortunately, Congress will not act unless the public applies enough pressure. A good beginning would be for truck drivers to abide by the speed limit and drive only in the right lane. Present laws should be enforced and stronger laws should be enacted for the safety of the public and the truck driver.

Anti-Lock Brakes ("ABS")

Antilock brake systems ("ABS") are designed to prevent a vehicle's wheels from locking during emergency braking on slippery roads. As the brakes are applied and the wheels slow down, an electronic control unit determines when any wheel is about to lock. The control unit then signals for reduced brake pressure, just enough to allow the wheel to start rotating again thus preventing lockup.

Vehicles equipped with ABS on all four wheels prevent skidding best. It allows you to steer while braking, helps you stop and accelerate. ABS only on rear wheels prevents the vehicle from spinning out of control, but front wheels may lock resulting in loss of steering control. When stopping on gravel, snow or slush allow more time for stopping distance. ABS does not necessarily stop sooner but it helps you maintain control during emergency braking situations.

Cars equipped with ABS can be more effective on slippery roads. A skidding wheel has less traction than a non-skidding wheel. ABS keeps wheels from skidding and also should stop wheels from locking.

On sheets of ice, wheels can lock at once. Therefore, drivers should practice threshold braking. Drivers who know this method can maintain better control of their vehicle. A skilled driver without ABS can possibly equal the performance on an average driver with ABS.

Threshold braking or limit braking is a technique where the driver adjusts control of the braking system in an attempt to maximize the braking force of the vehicle thus reducing the time and travel distance required to stop the vehicle. To put it more simply, every driver should know how to brake hard but to release pressure before vehicle stops. This should prevent brakes from locking.

If the ABS light inside your vehicle stays on, it means that your antilock brakes are not working. Have it checked, but remember if you use the brakes on a slippery road do not hold the brake down to the floor. Use your brakes as you would without ABS. Your regular brakes will be working.

An article in a newspaper questions the benefit of antilock brakes. In a study conducted by the Insurance Institute for

Highway Safety it was found that antilock brakes were not producing overall safety benefits.

However, two auto industry associates released a study stating that vehicles with antilock brakes had fewer accidents and injuries than those without them. This study showed an overall accident rate of nine to ten percent lower for cars with antilock brakes.

The insurance association declared that they did not know why antilock brakes are impressive on the test track, but not on the road. The answer could be that the drivers testing the antilock brakes know how to use them, but the majority of the driving public are not being instructed sufficiently by the auto agencies when the cars are purchased.

Motorists feel secure with antilock brakes because of impressive advertising by the manufacturers. However, in a survey, it was found out that most drivers had little knowledge of how this technology works. Forty-five percent of the owners of vehicles with antilock brakes thought the brakes should be pumped on slippery roads. It is apparent that misinformed drivers think they are safer because they have antilock brakes. Therefore, they may become careless or not allow enough space in front of them.

It appears likely that many accidents with the ABS are occurring because the driver either pumps the brake or removes the foot from the brake pedal too soon. If you use the antilock brakes in an emergency situation, you must exert a firm continuous pressure on the brake pedal. The brake will pulsate rapidly, which means the ABS is working. At this time, it is imperative that you do not remove your foot from the brake pedal.

Hold it down and do not pump the brake.

With standard brakes experienced drivers were accustomed to pumping the brake gingerly on slippery roads since a heavy foot would cause the car to spin out of control. Pumping antilock brakes could result in eliminating all braking power. When the antilock brakes are activated the system pumps the brakes faster than is humanly possible. Accordingly, the wheels unlock and the driver can retain steering control.

The effectiveness of antilock brakes has been enhanced by car commercials that imply that antilock brakes can prevent crashes because of better stopping power under all conditions. This is not completely true. On dry ground there is not much difference between standard brakes and antilock brakes. On slippery roads antilock brakes could make a difference. The Michigan State Police Traffic Crash Unit found that ABS equipped vehicles could not make hard cornering maneuvers while braking as well as vehicles with standard brakes.

Many drivers do not know how to use antilock brakes and the manuals that come with their car offer little help.

Pedestrians vs. Drivers

The only time most drivers yield to pedestrians when both have a green light is when an intersection is policed by an officer or school guard. If a pedestrian steps off the curb to cross the street under those conditions, the driver always must yield. Also, in business sections of large cities drivers usually yield only when groups of people are already crossing the intersection. Otherwise, when a person is walking on a green light, the driver will seldom yield.

Drivers making turns at intersections pose a dangerous threat to pedestrians, especially at night and more so if it is raining. When a driver and pedestrian have a green light, the driver must yield according to the law. Drivers must also yield to pedestrians at designated pedestrian crosswalks.

Many pedestrians are seriously injured or killed at night, especially on country roads. This is primarily due to roads that are poorly lit. When walking on country roads it is important to walk against traffic and to stay as far as possible from the driving lanes of the road. Wear lightly colored clothing and carry a flashlight or other type of light.

Conversely, if you are driving on a dark road, use the high beams unless a car is approaching and be watchful of pedestrians. They may not be easily visible especially if they are wearing dark clothing or have dark skin.

Hopefully, readers of this book will be vigilant and aware of this perpetual danger which kills or injures scores of people.

Position of "No Turn on Red" Signs

Unlike some stop signs, which face the wrong way by neglect, rectangular signs are usually posted securely to face the correct way. However, some drivers can be confused with signs which read "No Turn On Red." These signs must be facing you either on your side of the intersection or directly across the street facing you. If you come to an intersection and a "No Turn On Red" is not facing you but is facing east or west and you are going north or south, the sign is not for you. You must always stop first before you turn at a red light. Do not proceed if a vehicle is approaching or if people are walking.

Posted Speed Limits

A posted speed limit is the speed limit recommended under normal conditions. When driving during inclement weather or in extremely dark areas, drive slower in order to have control of your car. As you age, your night vision will be more affected than your day vision. Slow down at intersections so you will see the stop signs and find your way to your destination safely.

Seniors as well as all drivers must be watchful of children running out into the street, especially behind parked cars. If you observe children on the sidewalk, slow down and beep your horn lightly. Also, watch for balls or other toys in the street or rolling out into the street. There's a good chance a child will be following closely behind! If one child is chasing another one they often will run out into the street. If this is happening behind you or in front of you, pause to be sure they do not run in front of you. To maim or kill a child would be devastating and unforgettable. Total concentration is a necessity not only for seniors but for all drivers.

CHAPTER 3
Left Turns

Ah! Left turns - the ultimate nemesis of all drivers. If left turns were not permitted, a good percentage of all accidents would be eliminated. Just think of the multiple hazards drivers face when executing left turns in heavy traffic.

You could be smashed by a car coming towards you or a car behind you. As you wait in the middle of the intersection you are a sitting duck for drunks and people on drugs.

Watch for pedestrians when making your left turn.

Turning Left on Red

Many drivers are unaware that it is permissible to turn left on a red light when going from a one-way street to another one-way street (going to your left). Of course you must check traffic coming from your right and stop before making the left turn. Do not turn if a sign reads "No Turn On Red."

Left turns are more risky than right turns because of oncoming traffic. Many drivers, including seniors, do not know the correct way to make a left turn especially at a busy traffic light intersection.

A left turn can be executed safely in spite of the risks involved. When the traffic signal is green, you roll out slowly to the center of the street. Do not let any part of the car protrude into the oncoming traffic lane. Stay straight. Wait until you have space from the oncoming cars. Be sure that there are no cars coming towards you from the other lanes. If the oncoming traffic is extremely heavy you will have to wait until the oncoming traffic has stopped completely- this may require waiting until the traffic signal turns red. Turning on yellow could be very dangerous as it is not unusual for oncoming vehicles to speed through yellow and red lights. Before proceeding (even if the light has turned red) be sure that any oncoming traffic that is present has come to a stop.

Drivers making a left turn do not have the right of way unless they have a green left turn arrow. It is wrong for you to turn left as soon as the light changes to green if there are vehicles on the other side of the intersection waiting to proceed. It is also a violation if you are waiting for a red light to turn green and you turn left quickly just before the light changes to green. Both of these careless procedures can cause accidents. Many drivers are guilty of these infractions.

The Red Light Dilemma

A senior driver contacted me *via* email to inform me of a serious accident in which he was involved concerning a red light.

He wanted to execute a left turn at a busy intersection in which he made a drastic mistake which is common with new, some old and inexperienced drivers.

This is the situation: You want to turn left at a very busy intersection. When the traffic signal turns to green you correctly move to the center of the intersection. However, the traffic is so heavy that the light turns red and you are still waiting.

Now the problem is that this person who contacted me couldn't make the turn because four or five vehicles kept going through the intersection after the light had changed to red.

Now comes the fatal mistake. Instead of waiting until it was safe, he panicked and tried to turn. The result was a car crunching accident. Luckily no one was seriously injured.

In a situation like this do not be afraid to wait in the intersection while your signal light changes to red. Do not panic. The drivers at the intersection with the green light see you waiting to go. They are not moving. Although they may be annoyed, they will wait for you. I have been in this predicament many times and trust me you will manage to make your left turn safely. The rule to remember is never to turn left in any situation if vehicles are speeding towards you even if you are waiting a long time in the middle with your light on red. The drivers on your right and your left see what is happening. They realize that you can't make your left turn as long as speeding drivers go through the red light. Stay in the middle of the intersection no matter how long it takes.

Left Turns, Green Arrows and Green Lights

Many intersections have left green arrows but no sign which reads "Left Turn Signal." In this situation you may make the left turn on the green arrow and also on the regular green traffic signal when it is safe to do so. Some busy intersections have the regular traffic signals and also a sign which reads "Left Turn Signal." In this instance you are only permitted to exercise this left turn on the green arrow. This signal usually hangs in the center of the intersection. Drivers waiting to make a left turn cannot do it on the regular green light.

Suppose you want to make a left turn at an intersection and two drivers in front of you also want to make a left turn. When the light is green, both drivers go to the middle of the intersection to execute the left turn.

If they both are able to make the turn and the light turns red, you should not try to turn left on the red light. You should remain in your space (not in the intersection) and wait for the next green light.

However, when your green arrow appears, drivers coming towards you and at your sides may continue to move when their light turns red. These drivers are proceeding on your green arrow and drivers (possibly you) will also go when their green arrow expires.

Yield To Motorcycles

There is a very critical error that many drivers make that cause serious injuries and fatalities to motorcycle drivers. Countless numbers of these riders are being maimed or killed because of careless or ignorant drivers. A person riding a cycle cannot stop quickly or maneuver quickly without losing his balance. If you are making a left turn, do not do it if a motorcycle is coming towards you. Play it safe. Let the motorcycle pass you and then proceed. This type of accident should never happen, but unfortunately it continues unabated.

It would help if left turn arrows were installed in every busy intersection. Drivers wanting to turn left would only be permitted to do so on left green arrows.

The Departments of Transportation in all cities and large towns should review all traffic signals and make the necessary changes not only for left turns, but all signals and signs. If necessary changes were implemented, many lives would be spared. I don't think the City of Philadelphia has made important major changes for a number of years. This is probably true of most large cities.

Watching A Left Turn Accident Unfold

I was standing on the corner at the location of a popular restaurant near me when I witnessed an incredible traffic infraction.

This took place on a fairly busy intersection. A motorist facing me wanted to turn left to go into the restaurant. He had his left signal on. When his traffic signal was green, he did not move into the center of the street. He waited at the intersection until his traffic signal was red. I thought he would make the left turn immediately which is what many drivers incorrectly do. He compounded his misguided blunder by waiting a few seconds. I was stunned to see him try to make the left turn that late on red. A motorist on the intersection street in the meantime rightfully started to go. Both cars were going at the same time and the inevitable happened. Another left turn accident. The man who made the errant left turn was a senior citizen in his sixties, but he did not look senile and appeared to be in good condition.

This type of accident is happening thousands of times because motorists do not know how to safely execute left turns. This man was probably driving for forty or fifty years and unfortunately did not know how to make a left turn in traffic. Hopefully, he will learn by this unnecessary accident.

Watching this traffic disaster reinforced my opinion that many people driving for years never learned the proper method of turning left in traffic. There is no way to judge how many motorists today do not know how to execute left turns correctly. It would be pointless to estimate, but the number has to be astronomical.

A Left Turn Malaise

Almost every motorist is guilty of going through an intersection after a yellow light has changed to red. When you are about to cross an intersection and the yellow light appears, it is permissible to cross. However, it is customary for speeding drivers to pass red lights seconds after the yellow light changes to red. This illegal action creates a traffic hazard not only for the speeder and the one making the left turn, but also for other drivers close by.

This practice of drivers going through red lights is an endemic condition which exists nationally. There appears to be no solution unless cameras were placed on all busy intersections and more police were assigned to watch. This would be too costly so at the present time nothing more is being done and left turn accidents will continue to occur with costly consequences.

Almost every time I drive in heavy traffic, I encounter drivers who make left turns incorrectly. One day I was behind a vehicle in which the driver wanted to make a left turn. I also wanted to make a left turn. When the traffic signal turned to green she didn't move. The oncoming traffic was heavy and she evidently was afraid and didn't know how to cope with the situation. I got out of my car and approached the driver who was a middle-aged oriental woman. I explained the proper procedure to her. She gave me a blank stare, but when the light changed to green she followed my instructions and made the turn successfully.

There are countless numbers of seniors and others who do not know how to execute left turns in traffic. The result is many people are seriously injured. Years ago driving tests were easy. Many seniors were not taught properly. Many were self-taught. Left turns in traffic should be included in driving tests. It would also help if films were shown to teenagers in public schools and to people taking re-exams. However, this is not likely to happen. People will continue to be injured until some day all automobiles will have the technology to prevent accidents.

Do Not Get Moving Violations

If you commit a moving violation you will be assessed points. Different states have their own rules. Usually, if you are charged with a certain number of points, you will be asked to take a re-examination or you may lose your license. Although these tests are not difficult for drivers, elderly people dread the thought of taking them. Moving violations are usually the following:

- Entering the wrong way on a one-way street, turnpike, or limited access highway.
- Making a left turn where it is not permitted.
- Going through a red light.

- Going through a stop sign.
- Exceeding the speed limit.
- Reckless driving.
- Drunken driving.
- Being involved in an accident in which you are completely at fault.
- Driving too slowly especially on an expressway, turnpike, *etc.*

There may be other reasons but these are the most common. You do not get points for parking violations.

Important Rules for Seniors and Others

- Always carry an extra set of keys. Someday you will be glad you did.
- Never pass another vehicle at any intersection, curve or hill.
- If your car breaks down, pull over to the right, pull up your hood and put on your hazard lights.
- Never remove the cap from an overheated radiator. Wait for it to cool down and go to the nearest service station.
- Do not smoke while driving.
- Avoid alcoholic beverages before driving.
- Do not listen to the radio.
- A delayed green light means that the traffic signal for the cars coming towards you turns green before yours does- wait until your light turns green before proceeding.

- When two vehicles come to an intersection from different directions not controlled by a traffic signal, the one on the left should yield to the one on the right, but don't assume the other driver knows this rule and have an accident! The same rule applies to two way or four way stop signs. Otherwise, the one who clearly stops first goes first.

- If you approach a four way stop sign first, yield to any other driver if that driver is overly aggressive.

- If you are about to enter a traffic circle, you must yield to all vehicles already in the circle.

- To compensate for decreased depth perception, give yourself extra space.

- When driving, sit erect and hold the wheel firmly with two hands, one at ten o'clock and the other at two o'clock. Assuming this position will help to keep you alert. Rest your heel on the floor when using the accelerator, but not when you use the brake.

- Do not take your eyes away from the road for more than one or two seconds. Do not stare at billboards or anything on the sidewalk.

- Know how to get to your destination.

- When driving with others in the vehicle, do not engage in conversation with them.

- Senior drivers must make extra effort to stay focused since their motor skills and reflexes have declined with advancing years.

- Drive with low beams in daytime and in rain.

- Driving with lack of sleep can be as dangerous or more so than drunken driving.
- Coffee will not ward off fatigue or drunken driving.
- If possible, try to leave space around you to enable you to avoid a possible collision.
- Don't apply the brake pedal too long or hard when going down a steep hill as this could cause brake failure or "brake fade." Use a lower gear.
- A <u>Warning sign</u> alerts you to the changing conditions of a road. Warning signs are yellow or orange with black symbols and are usually diamond shaped.

Try this experiment: Go to a four-way stop sign intersection. Stand on the corner and watch the cars as they roll by the stop signs. You might have to watch about ten cars until you see one come to a complete stop. Evidently, some drivers think stop means slow down. One police officer could not write citations fast enough to cover all the violations. Most drivers brake, but do not stop. Many of them pass the stop sign as fast as ten miles per hour. However, at two-way stop signs, the drivers are more careful.

If you are ever requested to take a re-examination, be sure to come to a complete stop at all stop signs. Do not move until you count slowly to three. Not coming to a full stop is the single greatest reason people fail driving exams.

Two-Way Stop Signs

There was a time long ago when four way stop signs did not exist. Many residential areas are almost completely covered now with four-way stop signs. It is not uncommon to find an intersection with a two-way stop sign in the midst of an area replete with four-way stop signs. This could be dangerous. Some drivers are lulled into believing that all of the streets in the area have four-way stop signs only. Some four-way signs are not marked as such. Therefore, if you are approaching an unmarked stop sign, look at your left or right to see if the intersection street has the back shape of a stop sign. Do not assume that all intersections are four-way stop signs. Be alert and stay focused.

Drowsy drivers probably cause as many accidents as drunken drivers. Many drivers are so tired and sleepy that they close their eyes while driving. They feel that they will first rest their eyes for a few seconds. However, this habit is often fatal. Many times they do not open their eyes (especially at night) and the result is usually catastrophic and results in loss of life and property.

Four-Way Stop Signs

At a four-way stop sign, every street at the intersection has a stop sign. If two cars approach the intersection at the same time, the one on the right should go first. However, if two or three cars come to the intersection seconds apart, the one which stopped first should go first. Drivers should proceed in the order in which they stopped. If an aggressive driver goes before his turn, let him go. As an elder driver, you should have acquired wisdom to yield to pushy drivers.

Passing a Public Bus

When passing to the left of a public bus which has stopped near the curb to discharge passengers, pass carefully even though your traffic light is green. Sometimes people dash in front of buses without looking.

Just before you pass the bus, put your foot over the brake. Try to stay a few feet from the left side of the bus so you have some space to see better. Glance under the front of the bus so you might see if a person is running across the street in front of you. You could also tap your horn. Drivers and pedestrians make mistakes. Be ready for this type of pedestrian error. It could save someone's life.

Do not pass a trolley car on the right which has stopped to take on or discharge passengers, even thought the traffic light is green. Wait until the trolley starts to move.

CHAPTER 4
WOMEN DRIVERS

A long, long time ago women drivers were almost non-existent. When children playing in the street spotted a woman driver they would shout - "look out, woman driver."

In those days of the stick shift car without power steering, turning the wheel was not easy. It was almost impossible for the average woman to turn the wheel unless the car was in motion.

The stick shift gears of that era did not function as smoothly as modern stick shift cars. They stalled frequently unless the driver was experienced.

The modern women of today are not confronted with the obstacles faced by the women of yesteryear. The advent of the automatic transmission and power steering emancipated women forever. That change gave them the impetus they needed. Today, women drivers are everywhere.

Many women now in their sixties and seventies are not driving because they were afraid to drive a stick shift car or even an automatic transmission vehicle without power steering. As time went by some of their husbands developed health problems to the extent that some of them drove occasionally and some couldn't drive at all. This presented a dilemma to couples who were accustomed to driving to wherever they wanted to go.

Some husbands and wives had the foresight to prepare themselves for this difficult situation. Accordingly, some of the women learned how to drive. They became the ones who transported their husbands to doctors, did the shopping, *etc.* However, there were others who were unable to overcome their fear of driving. These women thought they were too nervous and were afraid to try. They believed that no one was as nervous as they and that they could not possibly learn to drive.

Well, I have news for them. I have personally taught thousands of older women and ninety percent of them succeeded. Some of those who did not succeed did not persevere. This included single older women and widows.

I am reminded of a widowed woman who took in and supported a homely, financially insecure man. When asked the reason why, she giggled and said, "he drives me everywhere and can even drive at night."

If you are in good health, you can learn to drive, be independent and perhaps be with a man because you are attracted to him.

If any woman reading this book is serious about driving, I suggest she read my book written especially for women entitled *"Drive Without Fear."* In it I give examples of twenty women who overcame their fear. If you tried once, try again. You will learn an easy way to master steering. Once you know how to steer precisely, you will be on your way to success.

My book can be ordered at thousands of bookstores and on the Internet at *Amazon.com*, Barnes & Noble and others. Go online to *Amazon.com* and read the five star reviews many women have posted.

A perfect example was a woman who came to me for advice. Her husband was schizophrenic and was getting worse. She was a nurse's aide at a hospital two miles away, but there was no transportation. She either had to walk to work or learn to drive.

Luckily she met a former student of mine who gave her my number. She had previously tried to learn from a well-known national driving school. She was told by two of their instructors that she would never learn.

It does not matter what driving school a person goes to if the instructor is not patient or knowledgeable. Instructors may pay more attention to some students more than other students for reasons that have nothing to do with their driving ability.

Her flaws were very evident. When making turns, she went too fast and her steering was not precise. True she was not a fast learner, but she was very determined. She had to learn. She had no relatives in the city having moved from New York when she was married. As in most cases when someone is motivated enough, she will survive and learn. Eventually she became an excellent driver and proudly told me afterwards that she drove to New York and back to Philadelphia.

Getting back to poor instruction, many a woman who tried to drive was never told to look straight ahead when driving. Aside from the fear of driving (which can be conquered), the inability to steer could be a major reason for women (or men) not driving. There are very few women or men whose motor skills are so subnormal that they can't learn. If a woman learning to drive looks at the front of the car or looks down at the ground, she will not stay in her lane. A novice, especially an older person who was never taught to look straight ahead into the center of the driving path will never learn how to steer correctly. The majority of young people who rode bicycles would look ahead without being told. As Columbo would say, "There's just one more thing." When driving, you should guide your body (your nose). Wherever your body goes, the car will go. Do not try to guide the car. If you watch the car, you will not be able to follow the road. Just look ahead into the center of your driving path. In the city, look about half - block to a block away. At a high speed , look further away. At speeds over fifty miles per hour, you should look ahead as far as your eyes can see, scanning the road up and down.

Steering is the key to driving. If you can learn to steer precisely, you can learn to drive. You must look straight ahead.

I may be prejudiced, but in my opinion the modern woman driver today is generally just as skillful as the male driver. When I was teaching male and female teenagers, I observed that many of the girls adapted to driving as well as the boys. Some of them surpassed the boys in skill and ability.

Women as a rule are more courteous and gracious than men and they will yield right of way more readily than men.

My opinion was reinforced recently when I was taking my daily walk. As I walked through a shopping center a young woman (in her late twenties) wanted to park, but she motioned for me to walk in front of her. Always a gentleman, I stopped and let her park first but not before she rewarded me with a warm, friendly smile. As I proceeded in the same parking area, I noticed an older woman trying to pull out of a parking space. She also stopped and waved me on. Again, I motioned for her to go and she also smiled at me graciously.

Later on I came to an intersection with white line crosswalks. As I was about to walk on the green light, another woman driver (in her forties) stopped over the white line. I could have crossed easily but with a disarming smile she went back a few feet so I could have more space to walk.

The three different encounters with these women happened very recently. It struck me how easily they smiled and how pleasant these incidents were. A young stud I am not. They smiled because they were kind and sweet.

In that classic movie of yesteryear, *"My Fair Lady,"* Rex Harrison sings the song, "Why Can't a Woman Be Like a Man." When it comes to driving an automobile I say, "why can't a man be like a woman?" Of course, many men are polite and courteous but when did you ever hear a woman shooting another person because of a driving argument! Road rage is a sickness almost non-existent with women.

Recently as I was waiting to walk across the street, I heard an incessant horn honking from a truck. An elderly woman was trying to turn left into the driveway of a bank which was located at the corner.

The speed limit on the street was twenty-five miles per hour. The truck was behind the woman. Evidently the truck driver wanted to reach the intersection before the green light changed to red.

The man did not let up with his horn. I could see him gesticulating angrily to his companion in the truck.

To her credit, she made the turn slowly, not allowing the truck driver to affect her driving. However, the loud horn blowing could have upset her and possibly triggered an accident.

The truck driver reaction to her slow turning was not an isolated incident. Many impatient drivers behave in this reprehensible manner because of their ignorance and lack of understanding.

I wonder if the truck driver would blow his horn so vehemently if the driver of the car in front of him was a powerful looking man. This is the attitude of many men who fancy themselves to be kings of the road.

It is sad but true that some drivers will never change. That is why there will always be automobile accidents.

Therefore, it is imperative for all senior drivers, especially women to not be intimidated by overbearing male drivers.

Females who learn to drive in their teens or twenties will usually continue to drive their entire lives. Many women who began driving in their middle age (forties or fifties) are the ones most likely to discontinue. It is likely that most of them had a fear of driving and after they obtained their driving license drove very little.

This happens more frequently with married women. They probably learned to drive late in life because of a fear of getting behind the wheel. The married couples who had two cars did not have this problem provided the woman drove the second car.

When there was no second car, the man usually drove and the woman did not insist on driving. Some men did not like when their wives drove as they felt it reflected negatively on their masculinity.

As time went by, circumstances changed. All too often husbands die or become incapacitated to an extent where they cannot drive anymore. For the past ten or twenty years, the woman had not been behind the wheel and now , in her late sixties or seventies, absolutely refuses to drive. Those women who continued to drive can now take their husbands to their medical appointments and can happily do the food shopping. In most instances these women started to drive at a young age so their husbands are fortunate. Otherwise, if the woman is too frightened to drive, the couple must depend on transportation available to seniors. The bottom line is that when a woman learns to drive in her middle years, she should not stop driving. If married, her husband should insist that she drive some of the time. If an unmarried women learns in her middle years, it is imperative that she continues to drive so she will be able to maintain her independence.

Women and Predators

You are a woman driving at night, alone on a freeway, expressway or limited access highway. You noticed that for the past ten minutes a dark car with a flashing blue light has been following you. Without warning the driver pulls up alongside you and motions you to pull over. He is wearing dark blue clothing with an emblem supposed to be a badge.

This is extremely important especially if you know you did nothing wrong. <u>Do Not Stop</u>. It's obvious the man is an imposter and a predator. Call 911 on your cell phone. Every woman who drives alone must have a cell phone. Start blowing your horn continuously. If he continues to follow you, get off at the next exit and head for a police station, convenience store or other public place. By using your horn non-stop, he will probably drive away. If possible, write down his license number. You must also report this incident to the police. If you can't get the license number, report the type of car, color, *etc.*

Perhaps the rapes and vicious killings that happen today are as numerous as in the past. It's possible that news stories are disclosed more freely today. However, women today must be vigilant and aware of the many mentally disturbed men who cannot control their evil impulses. The bottom line is that no woman driver should be gullible enough to stop her car. In today's society we should all be alert to guard against these vicious predators.

In June 2007 a man posing as a state trooper raped a woman in the back of his vehicle. After following her, he motioned for her to pull over. The woman foolishly obeyed him. This man was a *bona fide* predator who was looking for naive women to assault. His vehicle had a flashing light on the roof and he was wearing a gray uniform, dark pants and black boots. He was also carrying a gun. After the sexual encounter, he let her out of his car and drove away.

This tragic incident which happened in Pennsylvania exactly exemplifies the hazards women are subject to on the highways. She should not have pulled over to the shoulder and gone into his car. She should also have made noise with her horn.

CHAPTER 5
MALE DRIVERS

Sixty or seventy years ago, traffic conditions were not as complex as they are today. People did not drive as much; cars did not go as fast. Most women did not drive and there were fewer cars on the road.

As time went by and the number of cars and drivers multiplied, more roadways had to be built to meet the challenge. Building limited access highways, expressways and turnpikes connecting cities and towns became a necessity.

Driving on these new roadways was different than driving on city streets or towns. People had to adjust to a faster tempo in the new and vital traffic conditions.

Today trucks pose a hazard to others on the road. Truck drivers do not get enough rest, drive over the speed limit and habitually tailgate. Many of them use amphetamines to stay awake. Tractor-trailers overturn at an alarming rate. Either the driver falls asleep or goes too fast (which is especially dangerous on curves) when exiting the expressway, turnpike or limited access highway. It seems ironic that almost every time a tractor-trailer overturns it is carrying a flammable substance.

As male drivers age, their driving skills decline. Seniors who live into their eighties and nineties should evaluate their driving and act accordingly. Usually friends or relatives will warn you if they think your driving skill has slipped. To drive on the super highways you must be nimble and quick. If you are starting to feel uncomfortable when you are driving on these highways, perhaps you should consider avoiding them. There are always other roads to take you where you want to go. The time lost is inconsequential when measured against your life and the lives of others. We are not born with wisdom. It is acquired with age so be wise and make the right decision. Don't be like a friend of mine who always drove aggressively. He didn't change his driving behavior when he reached his seventies. After numerous inexcusable accidents and near misses, he changed his driving habits, concentrated more and his driving improved dramatically.

However, many men will not alter their habits of a lifetime and their driving privileges will be at risk. As time goes by and the number of people in their eighties and nineties increase, they will be under a microscope. It is inevitable.

Also under the spotlight will be the ones who become dangerous when they drive less than forty miles an hour on the speedways.

A viable solution would be to issue limited licenses for those slow drivers which would make it illegal for them to drive on super highways. Otherwise, many will continue to drive and perhaps cause loss of lives and/or damage to properties.

Octogenarians (mostly men) and older women should heed my warning if they want to protect their driving privileges. The thought of millions and millions of seniors on the roads in the coming years is scary to say the least. I also have a message for potential road-ragers. When a motorist cuts in front of you without warning and without enough space, don't take it personally. The perpetrator of those thoughtless and idiotic actions does not know you. He is doing this for any of the following:

1. He is not too bright.
2. He could be on drugs or intoxicated.
3. He does not have a license to drive.
4. He is completely thoughtless.
5. He thinks he is king of the road.
6. The man is an idiot.

Therefore, all you men who lose your tempers, think. Keep calm and don't resort to anti-social behavior and mayhem. I know of an instance when a reputable doctor chased someone who cut in front of him. When they both came out of their vehicles, the doctor was shot and killed by the other man who was incoherent and stupefied by drugs. The next time someone cuts in front of you laugh and forget about it. The person who cuts in front of you doesn't know you. In his mind he is speeding in front of a vehicle, not a human being.

The world is made of up all kinds of people. Most are decent and thoughtful. However, some are stubborn, impatient, angry, *etc.* There are all kinds on the road so driving will always be hazardous for the ones who obey traffic regulations.

Many men as a rule harbor a disdain towards female drivers. It's true that a long time ago women were novice drivers. As time went by women became more proficient but generally did not drive as aggressively as men. Without knowing the actual statistics, it is apparent that men cause more violent accidents than women and almost exclusively are responsible for road rage incidents.

Men beware. Women are on the rise. Latest statistics reveal that more younger women are attending universities than men. Girls' grades in elementary and high schools are surpassing boys' grades. Prevailing conditions do not remain stagnant. Women are gaining in political positions not only in the United States but also in major countries around the world. The current world trend indicates that women are gaining more power and it appears that this development will continue.

Los Angeles Drivers

Los Angeles may have the worst driving statistics in the United States. It is a city renowned for road rage, high-speed police chases and an antipathy for public transportation.

I have no doubt that its male drivers are the principal culprits. Running red lights is a way of life exacerbated by the use of cell phones.

Recently double-long buses were introduced in the San Fernando Valley with much publicity to alleviate the traffic problems of the city. Unfortunately, motorists have been crashing into these buses at an alarming rate, injuring many passengers. The county sheriff declared that up to that point, the driver of the car going through a red light caused every accident.

In my opinion, this sad situation in Los Angeles exists because of the attitude of its drivers. They drive with no patience and in most cases are extremely aggressive. However, they are not alone in their reckless habits. Other countries are guilty of the same traffic violations, among them are Italy and Israel. In Italy, it is common practice not to stop at stop signs and in Israel people drive like there is no tomorrow. I'm sure there are many males in Los Angeles who are careful, but a good portion of them drive irresponsibly. Seniors in Los Angeles should drive carefully within the speed limit to protect their driving privileges. The only solution to decrease the violations and to establish a new driving atmosphere is to inflict severe penalties on the traffic offenders. When this finally happens, seniors must be aware that they will come under close scrutiny and those with repeated offenses will be screened and not permitted to drive.

An elderly man in Los Angeles whose car hurtled through a farmers' marker killing ten people and injuring more than 70 was convicted of vehicular manslaughter with gross negligence – the harshest verdict possible.

The defendant, 89 and in poor health, could spend the rest of his life in prison for the 2003 crash. He faces up to 18 years in prison, but the judge could also sentence him to probation. Prosecutors would not say what penalty they would request. The defendant was not in court to hear the verdict.

His attorneys argued that he mistakenly stepped on the gas instead of the brake and panicked when his car raced into the open-air market. But prosecutors said he was careless to the point of criminal negligence and lacked remorse. It is very likely that when this type of accident continues to occur, senior drivers with driving infractions will be re-examined.

Other Tips

All senior drivers should always keep a cell phone in the car. You should belong to AAA or another agency, which provides aid if you have a problem such as a flat tire or mechanical failure. Many senior citizens are unable to physically or mentally handle car problems while on the road, so make sure you have the ability to call for help should the need arise.

My wife's uncle from New York paid us a visit. I sat next to him as he drove his car. We came to a corner where he wanted to make a left turn. The signal light was green but he did not go out to the middle of the street. We were in the first vehicle at the intersection. As soon as the light changed to red, he made the left turn. When I questioned him about it, he responded by telling me that he always made left turns that way.

What her uncle did was not an isolated case. He told me that he was driving for fifty-five years and that he was self-taught. In those days there were very few driving schools. Getting a license was much easier than today. These people who do not abide by safe driving rules (not purposely) are multiplying and in the years to come will possibly create hazards for everyone. It is inevitable that those unfit for driving safely will be weeded out for the safety of the public.

This is an item from the news on July 9, 2006. An 89 year old man drove his station wagon into a crowd at a summer festival in New London, Connecticut, injuring twenty-seven people, two seriously, city officials said. The accident happened during the city's Sail Fest Summer Festival.

This type of accident usually may unfortunately become more common in the future as more and more older Americans continue to drive into their 80's and 90's. The public will not stand by idly as these accidents proliferate. Seniors take notice. Concentrate on your driving every time or you will suffer the consequences.

I would like to mention that I received a notice in the mail from the Department of Transportation and it said, "Dear Motorist, you are required to undergo an eye and physical examination as part of the Pennsylvania Re-Examination Program, in accordance with section 1514 of the vehicle code. Drivers 45 years of age and older are randomly selected to participate in this program prior to the renewal of their driver's license to determine visual and physical qualifications necessary for the safe operation of a motor vehicle.

"To ensure the processing of your renewal application before your current license expires. The completed certificate must be returned to the bureau by the date indicated on the certificate."

Since my eyesight was good and I am physically sound, I was not apprehensive about retaining my license. However, if I failed their requirements, I am sure I would be called in for a driver's test.

There are other states which question senior's ability to drive as well as Pennsylvania. This is a first step to check the driving ability of older drivers. It is possible that eventually all seniors especially those with driving infractions or even minor ones will be called in for re-examinations.

Men Afraid to Drive

In the forty years I spent in the driver training field about sixty percent of my students were women of all ages. The older ones more than sixty years old were the most difficult. They had put off driving, some out of fear and others because their husbands always did the driving.

When a mature man didn't know how to drive, it was almost always because of an unnatural fear of getting behind the wheel. Of course these men claimed that they had no need to drive but down deep they wished they could drive. Of course some men tend to be timid and driving is one of their fears. However, circumstances in their lives changed which compelled them to try. Some of them had tried hypnosis or psychoanalysis but these treatments usually were not successful.

With constant encouragement I was successful in teaching most of them to drive. If a person has normal motor skills and adequate vision he or she should be able to master their fear and eventually obtain their goal. Conquering a fear such as driving is not easy but it can be accomplished. Millions and millions of people are able to drive so it can't be too difficult. This irrational fear can be overcome by having a positive attitude. When you finally get your license, you will have lingering fears for a while. Continue to drive and your nervousness and trepidation will diminish. Once this roadblock is eradicated, you will be a happier person.

CHAPTER 6
TIPS FOR THE ELDERLY

School Buses

When a school bus stops with flashing red lights on the top of the bus, you must stop at least ten feet from the bus. It does not matter from what direction you are coming, you must stop. If your traffic light is green you must stop. If you are coming from the side intersection, or if you are coming towards the bus, you must stop. When all of the children reach the pavement and the bus proceeds to move, you may also move provided the top red lights are not flashing. You may go when you are on the other side of a divided highway. A divided highway is a two-way street divided by an island or a median strip. However, do not go even under this condition if there are children still crossing the street. Children do not know these rules. They may continue to walk through the median strip if it is not a physical barrier. Do not move until they cross the street.

Letting Cars Out of Driveways

You are driving on a busy street with shopping sections and lots of driveways. As you are driving you notice many drivers waiting at the driveways for the opportunity to exit. Should you stop or should you continue? According to the rules, the driver of the car in the driveway should wait until the way is clear. Some good-hearted drivers stop and let these cars go out onto the street. If the traffic is bumper to bumper and the cars are moving a few feet at a time, you can allow a car to get in front of you. However, if the traffic is moving smoothly at twenty miles per hour or more, it could be hazardous to stop in the middle of the street. You could get hit in the rear. If you want to be a good samaritan and let someone in, be sure the car in back of you is not near you and not moving too fast. Do not stop unless you are positive it can be done safely. My advice is not to stop.

Letting Pedestrians Walk in Front of You

Do not tell pedestrians to walk in front of you when they have a red light. If you want to allow a pedestrian to walk in front of your car you must be one hundred percent positive that there are no other cars coming into your intersection. Sometimes a car will be turning into the very area that the pedestrian is walking. It is better for pedestrians to wait until it is legally safe to cross the street. If someone wants to cross in the middle of the street, it could be dangerous for you to stop especially if other cars are speeding behind you. If you notice an elderly person walking in the middle of the street, not looking left or right, be careful. Pump your brake a few times so that the driver in back of you knows you are stopping and motion for other drivers behind you to slow down. It is also advisable to tap your horn lightly to alert the elderly person and the other drivers.

Vision Problems

Color Blindness: This is a trait inherent more in men than women. The top traffic light is always red, the middle light is always yellow and the bottom light is always green.

Peripheral Vision: This is the ability to see to the sides while looking straight ahead. Some people's field of vision is better than others. Most people have a field of vision of approximately one hundred and eighty degrees. This means their peripheral vision is ninety degrees on each side. A driver's peripheral vision should be at least one hundred and forty degrees.

Tunnel Vision: Some people can only see straight ahead. They have very little or no side vision at all. These people are at a great disadvantage when driving. People with tunnel vision or below average peripheral vision should reduce speed at points where anything could be approaching from the sides. It is necessary for these people to turn their heads more at intersections or points of merging traffic. If you have tunnel vision or poor peripheral vision, let an ophthalmologist advise you about whether it is safe for you to drive.

Know The Traffic Scene Around You: If there is nothing wrong with your eyes, do not drive as if you are in a tunnel. Your peripheral vision should pick up any movement on your sides. You cannot drive safely for too long if you are oblivious to the cars behind you and on your left and right side. However, you should not stare in the mirror. Quick glances in the mirror are best. Sometimes a quick turn of your head, especially to the right is helpful. The best way to see a car over your right shoulder is to turn your head quickly. Be sure not to turn the wheel inadvertently when taking your quick glances.

Emergency Vehicles

When you hear a siren or see a vehicle with flashing lights behind you, pull over to the right if possible and stop. There will be times when you will not be able to pull over to the right. You will have to do what is best under the circumstances. Sometimes you have to move to the left to allow the emergency vehicle to get through. Other times you may not move at all. In situations like this, it is always better if you stay in the right lane. The right lane is the safest place to be for all slower drivers.

Do Not Overreact

A middle-aged driver may have a tendency to overreact under certain situations. Be very careful not to jam the brake unless you must avoid hitting something or someone. If you pay attention to your driving you should never have to jam the brakes unless an animal or person darts in front to you. When you are about to cross an intersection do not panic when it appears that another car is not stopping on your left or right. If you are observant, you will know if the intersection is controlled by a four-way or two-way stop sign. For an inexperienced driver it may appear that the other driver is not stopping. Always be aware of the danger involved when you slam on the brake. You could cause a rear-end collision.

The safe procedure is to place your right foot over the brake and glance quickly towards the car. If the car continues to move, tap the horn and slow down or stop if necessary. The driver behind you should see what is happening and should slow down. The bottom line is think before you jam the brake pedal.

Watch For Pedestrians

Almost half of all pedestrians killed or injured in traffic are struck down at night. The problem is compounded when they are wearing dark clothing, especially in the rain.

If you have impaired hearing, be alert and never close your windows completely. Be especially aware of emergency vehicles.

After a snowstorm clean the headlights and exhaust pipe.

Do not let drivers behind you try to force you to pass yield signs when it appears risky. Let them honk!

When starting out from a parked position, always check the rear first.

Sport Utility Vehicles

Although the disadvantages outweigh the advantages, many people prefer to drive SUV's. In an SUV, you sit higher and have a better view of the traffic scene ahead. Most of them have four wheel drive so they have better traction in slippery weather. Since the headlights are higher than the average sized car, you must use the low beam when cars are approaching. The glare from your SUV would especially bother seniors in oncoming traffic. It seems that SUV's caught people's attention because they were an innovation not seen before. Now that gas prices have skyrocketed perhaps their sales will diminish, as they are gas-guzzlers.

Most of them are built on a truck frame so they have a higher center of gravity and have a tendency to rollover. You must brake sooner and leave an adequate space cushion for stopping safely when driving an SUV. SUV's do not handle as easily as passenger cars.

Women's spatial and depth perception is inferior to that of men. An SUV does not corner as easily as a passenger car so women would be inclined to make wider turns. It is obvious that some women would be better off if they did not drive SUV's, but SUV'S appear to be here to stay.

Lately the buying trend seems to be moving away from the traditional SUV. Auto manufacturers are streamlining the SUV making them more attractive by changing the exterior to look more like a traditional sedan or station wagon.(the "crossover")

The Following Statements are True or False

1. Older people have the same reaction time as younger people.

2. Impatience on the part of motorists can cause accidents.

3. Normal reaction time is three fourths of a second.

4. There are more accidents in dry weather than in rainy weather.

5. Tires will be more likely to hydroplane when they are bald.

6. A small amount of alcohol will not affect your driving.

7. Most accidents are caused by mechanical failure.

8. Drivers between the ages of fifty and sixty have better driving records than those between eighteen and twenty-five.

9. Drivers over eighty have more accidents than those between fifty and sixty.

10. If you are driving at forty miles an hour, it will take about sixty feet to stop.

11. Since all cars are equipped with turn signals, it is not necessary to know the hand signals.

12. If another driver is tailgating you, slow down.

13. An icy road is more slippery at a temperature of 10 degrees than 32 degrees.

14. Always carry a can of gasoline in your car for emergencies.

15. If you cannot afford liability car insurance, drive very carefully so you won't have an accident.

16. Drivers over sixty-five are increasing three times as fast as the general population.

17. Odd numbered route signs go north and south and even numbers go east and west.

Answers to True or False

1. False: As you get older your reaction time gets slower.
2. True
3. True
4. False: Accidents can happen at any time.
5. True
6. False, and remember that women and seniors may become more impaired with a given amount of alcohol ingestion.
7. False
8. True
9. True
10. False: It will take about 150 feet to stop.
11. False: If your turn signals are defective, you must use hand signals.

Left Turn   Right Turn   Stop

12. False: Slowing down may incite the other driver. Maintain the normal speed for the road and move out of the way when it is safe to do so.
13. False: An icy road is more slippery at 32 degrees.
14. False: A driving emergency may cause an explosion.

15. False: Do not drive if you cannot afford liability insurance. If you are ever involved in an accident, you could be in serious trouble.
16. True
17. True

Railroad Crossings

Always slow down when approaching a railroad crossing. You must never try to beat the train if the red lights are flashing. Stop at least fifteen feet away from the tracks.

If the railroad crossing has no lights or crossing gates, proceed with caution. After the train has passed, check both directions. Do not start to cross the tracks until a car in front of you has cleared the tracks.

If your car ever gets stuck on the track and you can't get it started, leave your car and try to notify 911.

Crashes occur at railroad crossings all the time because of driver impatience, inattention, drowsiness and a lack of common sense. Usually a warning sign is placed in view well before a railroad crossing.

Braking Not Always Best

Using the brake is not always the answer to avoiding an accident. I was giving a nervous older woman a driving lesson one day in her car. I didn't like to teach people in their cars, but because she had a license I made an exception. I also had previously given her a few lessons in my dual control car.

As we were starting to cross an intersection (residential) on a green light, I noticed a car approaching on our right that didn't seem to be slowing down. The car was not going fast, but appeared to be moving closer to us at a steady speed of about twenty miles per hour. It was obvious to me that this driver was not going to stop. If I told my student to brake, we would be struck broadside. I quickly told her to step on the accelerator, which fortunately she did. She didn't step on it hard enough and our car was nicked slightly.

A police car came by. We told him what had happened. He raced after the vehicle and apprehended him. We found out that the driver was arrested for driving under the influence of drugs.

There is one more thing to do besides stepping on the accelerator to avoid an accident. If there is nothing on your left or right, you can steer away from the vehicle, person or animal you wish to avoid. In this instance, you must be aware of the space around you before you make a move.

Brake Failure

If your brakes fail, shift to a lower gear and pump the brake pedal rapidly. If that is ineffective then step on the emergency brake (not abruptly). Hold onto the brake release handle so you can release the emergency brake if the rear wheels lock and you begin to skid. As you slow down, drive off the road, put on your hazard lights and try to stop.

If you have the lever type emergency brake, keep your thumb on the control knob and don't pull up the lever too abruptly. Follow the same procedure as explained for the foot pedal emergency brake.

Stalling

If the car stalls, hold the wheel tightly as you will have trouble turning the wheel. Shift to neutral (never park) and try to start the engine. If the car doesn't start, press the brake hard. If you have power brakes they will lose their power. Try to go off the road and turn on the hazard lights.

Headlight Failure

If your headlights suddenly go out, slow down immediately and carefully pull over to the side of the road or off the road. Sometimes by trying the other light switches the headlights may go on again. Therefore, try the high beams, parking lights, hazard lights or turn signals.

If you keep your car in good condition and have your mechanic check it regularly you will decrease the chance of a mechanical failure in your vehicle.

Facing a Rise in Hit-And-Run Accidents

One of the most frightening statistics involving America's 198 million licensed drivers is that hit-and-run accidents have increased by 20 percent since the year 2000.

Philadelphia has experienced a number of hit-and run accidents recently. In fact, several older people have been hit while trying to make it across wide streets with fast-moving traffic. Many of them have trouble judging distance or fail to realize how fast the approaching traffic is moving.

Roosevelt Boulevard in Philadelphia is one of the widest streets in the city and has been the scene of some of these accidents. A nun was killed there in a hit-and-run not so long ago. Since then, a grandmother was injured while crossing this road with her 7 year old grandson, who was struck and killed.

Such crimes are among the most difficult to solve because they often occur after dark and in many cases there are no eyewitnesses.

Last year, 4,881 pedestrians were killed on America's roads and highways. Nearly one-fifth, or 974, died in hit-and-runs according to the National Highway Traffic Safety Administration.

There has been a 2 percent increase in the number of pedestrians killed since the year 2000. But in the same period deaths by hit-and-runs increased almost tenfold. Experts often have trouble explaining the increase in fatalities, but generally attribute the deaths to the increased number of cars and pedestrians on America's roads. In addition, many drivers are believed to be distracted while using telephones, adjusting car radios, or talking with their passengers.

In 2003, nearly 1,500 pedestrians were killed by hit-and-run drivers. Some drivers were unaware they had even hit a pedestrian, but others fled because they were frightened on facing the consequences. Those fears increase when the driver has been drinking.

An analysis by the AAA Foundation for Traffic Safety showed that about 11 percent of all police-reported crashes involve a hit-and-run driver, and that pedestrians make up the majority of the victims.

Those accidents are only a microcosm of what may occur in the years ahead when the number of senior drivers increases tremendously as people continue to live longer. Foretelling the future is uncertain, but logic and human history should not be disputed. Driving accidents caused by seniors will certainly increase.

About 60 percent of the people killed in hit-and-run crashes are pedestrians. Statistics show that 58 percent of fatal hit-and-runs occur on Friday, Saturday or Sunday, and 47 percent occur between 9:00 p.m. and 3:00 a.m.

The best way for pedestrians to avoid being a hit-and-run victim is to be an alert pedestrian.

The following are tips to help keep senior pedestrians safe:

- Obey traffic signals.
- Look left, then right, and left again before crossing the street, even when in a crosswalk.
- Remain alert and aware of cars as they approach and pass you.
- Do not assume drivers see you because you see them.
- If walking at night, wear reflective and light-colored clothing and carry a flashlight.

The Meaning of Yellow Lines

It is important to know that yellow lines divide traffic moving in opposite directions. It could be a broken yellow line, a solid yellow line or a double solid yellow line. You may not cross a solid yellow line except to turn left at an intersection or to enter a driveway.

You may change lanes only when the broken line next to the solid line is on your side. You may change lanes on a road with broken lines when it is safe to do so.

The Meaning of White Lines

Roads marked with white lines indicate traffic moving in the same direction. Broken white lines can be crossed. Solid white lines should only be crossed sparingly, when necessary.

The space to the right of a solid white edge line can be used for repairs. This edge line on the right can also be used as a guide at night when an approaching vehicle's high beams obscure your vision.

"I always straddle the white line, just to be safe."

CHAPTER 7
ACCIDENT-FREE DRIVING

Stay In Your Lane

When you are driving on a boulevard or multi-lane highway, you must not stare at passing vehicles. Staring at passing vehicles on either side gives you the illusion that they are running into you. Remember that quick one-second glances are all you need to check the sides. Otherwise, you should be looking straight ahead into the center of your lane. Do not change your lane unless it is necessary.

Check Traffic Before Changing Lanes

Never change lanes unless you are certain you can do so without interfering with another driver. Before looking in either mirror, set your position on the road so you will not weave. Do not move the wheel while looking in the mirror. When you can see that you are guiding the car correctly, take a quick glance in the rear mirror. Look again in front of you to observe the traffic scene. To move over to your left, look in the rear mirror for a second. Now glance in the left side mirror and if the driver behind you is not trying to change lanes to the left, you can execute your lane change safely.

Before you move over to the lane on your left, put on your left turn signal. Be sure to look in the center of the lane you are entering approximately ten to twenty yards away. If another vehicle is ahead of you, look towards the center of it.

Do not use the brake when changing lanes. Maintain your speed. When you change lanes there should be no vehicle behind you on your left for at least five car lengths. Also try to judge the speed of the vehicle alongside of you. If the vehicle appears to be moving much faster than you, let him pass before changing lanes. Always look twice before you make your move. Do not forget to cancel your turn signal after you have changed lanes.

Moving over to the lane on your right can be more difficult because of the blind spot on the right side. Of course, you must look in the rear mirror following the same procedure as explained for going into the left lane. Glance, do not stare. Before moving over to the right, you must turn your head quickly over your right shoulder to see if a car is on your right side. Again, be sure to signal before moving over and do not brake while doing so. Do not move to the right lane until no car is in the right lane behind you. Remember this very important rule – NEVER, EVER MOVE THE WHEEL TO THE LEFT OR TO THE RIGHT WITHOUT LOOKING BEHIND YOU. Many an accident happens when a driver absent-mindedly turns the wheel without checking the rear.

Some senior drivers in their eighties do not like to admit that their driving skills have declined. Others do not realize that they are not the drivers they once were.

Drivers changing lanes cause many accidents. Errant left turns and changing lanes are two major causes of serious accidents in every civilized country. Changing-lane accidents may be caused by lack of concentration, negligence, ineptitude, slow reflexes or deteriorating reaction time.

Every senior driver must realize his or her own shortcomings. If you do not feel confident about changing lanes particularly on expressways, turnpikes, *etc*, do not try. You are probably retired now and time is not an issue. Play it safe and stay in your lane except when it absolutely necessary to change lanes.

Do Not Stare at Distractions

Many older drivers have a tendency to have "sticky" eyes when a distraction appears. Remember never to take your vision away from the driving path in front of you for more than a second at a time. You must learn to take quick glances at any distraction but your eyes must always go back to the road in front of you. If something unusual is happening in front of you, put your foot above the brake pedal. Look in the mirror quickly. Do not jam the brake suddenly. The best drivers know how to glance quickly without staring. Many rear-end collisions occur when the driver suddenly jams the brake. Many others occur when the trailing driver is distracted and fails to notice that the driver in front of him has slowed down or stopped. Rear-end collisions in most instances are avoidable yet they are probably the most common of all accidents.

You Could Steer Incorrectly or Brake at the Wrong Time and Cause an Accident

When driving you must not let your mind wander. Concentrate only on your driving so your eyes and your brain can work together in coordination as a team. Give your brain the right message and your hands will guide you correctly.

Anticipate Problems

An intelligent, skillful driver must be aware of impending traffic problems before they happen. Aggressive drivers do not allow for the mistakes of others. The aggressive driver has no patience. In many situations, skill will not compensate for aggressive driving. Lack of patience by many drivers is the cause of many automobile tragedies.

A knowledgeable driver should be able to sense what another driver is about to do. Assume you are driving on a busy boulevard. A vehicle on your left is crowding the vehicle in front of it. This driver is moving aggressively, but the driver in front of him is impeding his progress. It is obvious that this aggressive driver is looking for a way to pass. At this point, you should realize that this aggressive driver may try to pass by moving in front of you. Check the traffic behind you and tap your brake lightly to warn the driver behind you that you are slowing down. As soon as the aggressive driver sees you leave a space, he will move in front of you and pass. When driving on boulevards or highways, this situation will happen frequently. Be ready for it.

Driving in Snow, Rain and at Night

Many people avoid driving in the snow, but sometimes it is necessary. Other times it may start snowing while you are driving. If possible, try to avoid driving while it is snowing. Besides the hazard of slippery roads, poor visibility in the front and rear could pose a serious problem.

The best vehicle in the snow is, of course, a four-wheel drive vehicle, especially a four-wheel drive sports utility vehicle (SUV). These vehicles will do better in deep snow or deep water as they are built higher from the ground.

Equip your car with good snow tires. If you have a front wheel drive car, put the snow tires on the front wheels. A good idea is to put all-season mud and snow tires on all four wheels. Under no circumstances should you drive in the snow with worn out tires. This is asking for trouble. If you drive carefully and with intelligence, you will be able to drive in the snow. However, there are certain times when no one should be driving. When the streets are unusually icy, stay where you are and do not drive.

If you are driving a rear wheel drive car, load your trunk with approximately two hundred pounds of weights. This will give you better traction in the snow or rain. Before driving in the snow, be sure to have a full gas tank so your fuel line will not freeze and so that you will not have to worry about running out of gas. Also, fill the windshield washer reservoir. If your exhaust pipe is immersed in snow, be sure to clear it out before driving.

This could cause carbon monoxide to escape into the car possibly causing serious health problems or even death. When planning a trip in snowy terrain, take along a small shovel, flashlight, rock salt, sand or ashes. Kitty litter can also be tossed under your tires to increase traction.

To help you drive safely in snow and ice, you should drive slowly and brake gently. Allow plenty of space between you and the car in front of you. To avoid a loss of traction, a driver must know how to ease up on the brake before it locks. Practice braking on an empty lot to test your brakes and improve your skill. Pressing too hard on the gas pedal especially from a stopped position can also cause loss of traction and wheelspin.

The slower you are driving, the less you will skid. Take your foot away from the brake. If you panic and jam the brake, the skid will worsen. When the car skids, the tires are sliding. The idea is to get them to start revolving, so that you can steer the car.

Your car will not skid as easily on soft fluffy snow. It will skid more when the sun puts a glaze on the ice. When you drive slowly on ice and do not press the brake hard, you will not skid as much. However, if you are caught in bad weather and your car skids, do not panic. Always turn the wheel in the direction of your skid. For example, if the back of the car starts to slide towards the right, turn the wheel to the right. If the back of the car starts to slide towards the left, turn the wheel to the left or turn the wheel in the direction you want the front to go. If you are driving slowly, you will be able to stop safely. Skidding is dangerous when the car is moving too fast and you press the brake too hard.

If you are starting out on ice and your wheels keep spinning, do not press hard on the gas pedal. You can burn out the transmission and your tires. If the car does not move forward, try to carefully go backwards (place transmission into "reverse ") Move the wheel so you can get the tires on a different track. Try moving back and forth until you get out. However, if you are still stuck on the ice, put sand, chains, or any substance to melt the ice under the tires. What you **<u>should not do</u>** is put the car in first gear (low gear).

Low gear will increase the tendency of the wheels to spin, especially on slippery surfaces like ice, snow and rain-covered roads. In fact, if you have a manual transmission, start out in second or third gear to help get the car moving and to minimize the tendency of the wheels to spin.

If you are driving on an icy street and you know you have to stop at the intersection, try to use the brake on the least icy section of the street. If you are turning in the snow, use the brake gently before you make the turn. Always look in the center of the lane as you turn. This follows that hard and fast rule I advocate strongly – "Look where you want to go."

Do not pump the brake if your car has anti-lock brakes (ABS). Simply press the brake and hold it down and the ABS system will do the pumping for you. If you do not have anti-lock brakes, pump gingerly.

If you are ever driving on an icy road, there is something you can do that might help stop the car more easily. Usually the car skids when the brake is pushed too hard, but sometimes if the ice is very slippery you may skid slightly even though you apply gentle pressure. When you see a stop sign or a red signal light, put your indicator lever into Neutral ("N") about ten or fifteen feet before your stop. In "N" the engine is disengaged from the transmission and the car can be stopped easier since the engine is not pulling the car. When you are ready to go simply put the lever back into Drive ("D") and start out slowly.

Rear-End Collisions

Rear-end collisions are the most prevalent and most preventable of all types of vehicle accidents. The greatest obstacle to resolving these world-wide disasters is the human species. At the top of the list is the drunken driver, male or female, who destroys his/her own life in addition to killing or maiming innocent victims. Unfortunately, rear-end collisions are a problem without a foreseeable solution.

Truck drivers are responsible for many rear-end crashes with the most calamitous results. Truck drivers have demolished motionless automobiles in broad daylight on state turnpikes and highways. Many truck drivers speed to make more deliveries and do not get enough sleep or rest. Young people who inflict rear-end collisions on unsuspecting victims are usually guilty of excessive speed, impatience, and inattention, especially when distracted by other teenagers in the vehicle. Imbibing alcoholic liquids is also a factor.

Every day drivers commit mayhem on the highway because they momentarily look away from the traffic scene in front of them. People who have been driving for many years sometimes tend to become complacent or careless.

There is a stigma attached to a senior citizen if he or she is the perpetrator in a rear-end collision. The popular opinion of most people is that older people should not drive. As people get older, reaction time becomes slower and their vision worsens. Accordingly, it is incumbent for them to be focused at all times to compensate for their shortcomings.

Driving in the Rain

Every time it rains the accident rate increases because people continue to drive as if the ground were dry. I do not think that most older drivers are guilty of driving too fast on wet roads. Speeding over puddles of water causes the car to hydroplane. When this happens the car skims on the water and steering and braking become ineffective because the car's tires are not in touch with the roadway. Driving on gravel and mud can also be hazardous. Drive slowly and do not jam the brake pedal under these conditions.

Although driving in the rain is less hazardous than driving in the snow, the rules are similar. You will not skid as easily as you would in the snow but you should use the brake pedal gingerly. If you press hard on the accelerator from a standing still position, your wheels may spin.

Be careful at the beginning of a rainfall. The rain activates the dry oil on the ground making it slippery. Be sure to leave extra space between you and the car in front of you. Do not brake hard and do start out slowly. When driving on a highway during a heavy rain, try to avoid the far left hand lane because of the risk of water being thrown onto your windshield by vehicles coming towards you. This could cause a complete loss of visibility which could be dangerous or fatal.

Good visibility is especially important in inclement weather. If your defroster is not doing the job, turn on the air conditioner. This will clear all of your windows. When driving in the daytime, during heavy rain, put on your low beam headlights.

Space Cushion

Never tailgate. Try to keep a safe following distance from the car in front of you. If the driver in front of you stops suddenly, you may not be able to stop in time. Tailgating interferes with the field of vision in front of you. At a speed of thirty miles per hour, stay three car lengths away from the car in front of you. At forty miles an hour, stay about five or six car lengths away. When you are driving fifty miles an hour or more or in bad weather, you should increase your following distance. The rule of one car length for every ten miles per hour would not be sufficient. The problem with increasing your following distance is that other drivers will pull in front of you and shorten your following distance. This irresponsible behavior violates one of the most critical tenets of safe driving but it is prevalent on every road.

Reaction Time

The time it takes to make a decision and act on it is called reaction time. Normal reaction time is one half to three fourths of a second. As we get older our reaction time gets longer. That is reason enough for seniors not to speed. The faster you drive, the less time you have to think and act.

Night Driving

Many older people cannot see too well at night. Do not drive at night if your eyes cannot penetrate the darkness. If you are not sure, get an eye examination. At twilight put on the low beams. High beams are used on very dark roads when no cars are coming towards you. If a car is coming towards you for less than five hundred feet, switch back to low beams as high beams could blind the driver coming towards you.

It is more difficult to drive at night because of the decreased visibility. When it is raining at night, the problem is compounded because of the glare from the wet streets and the water in the air. If a car is coming towards you with high beams, glance towards the right edge of your lane. Do not look at the headlights of the oncoming car. On a foggy day or night, always use low beams.

Driving at night is more tiring than driving during the day. If you go on a trip at night, plan to stop and rest your eyes.

Drive Right at Night

- Slow Down
- Take a Second Look
- Avoid Glare
- Use Lights Properly
- Increase Following Distance

Driving Tips

If you have a tire blowout, the car will swerve. Let up on the accelerator. Do not jam the brake and do not turn the wheel abruptly. Hold the wheel firmly and try to keep the car straight. Brake gently and pull over to the shoulder.

You are going straight waiting for a red signal to change to green. A driver facing you wants to make a left turn. Traffic is heavy. Do not motion this driver to turn left in front of you. You are not a traffic officer. You are not doing this driver a good turn. If this person listens to you and turns left without observing oncoming traffic, a serious accident may occur. Play it safe and let the other driver follow the rules of safe driving.

When you are the first one at an intersection waiting for the green light, do not start out the second the light turns to green. Look left and right for a second or two to be sure that no one is speeding through the red light. There are many reckless drunk drivers who habitually go through red lights seconds after the green light changes to red.

Hidden Stop Sign

Suppose you are approaching an intersection controlled by a stop sign. The sign on your right is hidden. If you look diagonally from your right side to the other side you can see the back of a stop sign. Now you know that you have a stop sign on your right.

Don't be a Horn Blower

What is it that makes some drivers honk their horns constantly at everything that displeases them? There are all kinds of people in the world and consequently there are all kinds of drivers. It is curious that most horn blowers are men.

The impatient driver has adopted this outrageous practice over his entire driving career. He uses the horn as a way of bullying other drivers. There are some older drivers who may be timid and do not drive as fast as other motorists. The intelligent, understanding driver will wait patiently for the opportunity to pass the slow driver.

There is a time when it is proper to use the horn. The primary purpose of the horn is to warn another motorist or pedestrian who might not see you. The horn is to be used gently except for an emergency.

If a driver is alert and focused, he or she can prevent an accident with skillful driving and not with unnecessary use of the horn.

Potholes

Do your best to avoid going over potholes or jagged crevices. Be alert and always scan the road up and down. If you see the pothole, try to avoid it but check the traffic to the sides and rear. If you cannot possibly avoid it, reduce your speed but do not cause a rear-end collision. It may not be safe to brake too abruptly.

If the impact is severe, you may suffer a flat or cut tire. Air can also seep from the tire by the force of the hubcap or wheel cover against the rim.

The bottom line is that when you are behind the wheel, pay strict attention to your driving and do not get distracted.

If Key is Stuck and Wheel is Locked

One day while relaxing at home I received a frantic telephone call from my wife who had been out shopping with a few friends. "I can't start the car" she exclaimed! The key is stuck and the steering wheel is locked.

After telling her to calm down, I told her to be sure the key was in all the way. Next I instructed her to rock the wheel back and forth gently and at the same time turn the key. Also, be sure to press the brake, while doing this.

She called me back a few minutes later and happily informed me that after following my advice, the key turned and the wheel unlocked.

This situation happens infrequently, but it can occur if you drive often. If it happens to you, do not panic. Simply follow the above procedure and the problem will be solved.

Flashing Lights

It is hard to believe that many people drive for years and do not know what flashing red and yellow lights mean. For those who are unsure, here it is:

A flashing red light means stop and only proceed when it is safe-it should be treated like a stop sign

A flashing yellow light means proceed with caution only if the way is clear.

A flashing yellow light has the right of way over a flashing red light.

The Driver Behind You

I have been driving for many, many years and I believe that my feelings when I am behind the wheel are shared by many other drivers.

When I am driving on the road, I feel very comfortable when no vehicle is behind me. I can drive my way with no distractions. There are times when I make the mistake of trying to accommodate other drivers, particularly the ones to my rear.

Of all the driving infractions the one that infuriates me the most is the driver who drives too fast behind me, tailgating me persistently. There are some times when I wrongly drive faster to oblige the speeder.

The correct procedure is to drive at the speed limit and not let the person driving behind you influence your driving. Move out of the tailgater's way as soon as it is safe to do so. Do not slow down suddenly or he may strike the rear of your car. Ironically this person will usually be angry and his or her driving will reflect his/her demeanor. It would be very rare for a speeding tailgater to be a female. Women are innately different than men. The usual violator is usually a male between the ages of twenty one to forty. This is only my opinion, but I cannot be too far off the mark.

Some drivers tailgate habitually. To ask them why they drive this way would be fruitless. We cannot ignore them since they involve us with their unsafe driving practices and unfortunately we have to know how to deal with them.

There is no solution to speeding drivers. There is something in their psyche that drives them to behave this way. At any rate, these people are hazards on the road. Some day in the not too distant future, vehicles will drive by themselves and the malignant situation will be terminated. Today, Lexus already has a car which parks by itself.

Decisions

Is anything more important than making the right decision while driving? Faulty decisions by drivers have caused countless injuries and fatalities. Young people make wrong decisions because of recklessness. Old people (eighty or more) may not be capable of the right decision because of hearing difficulties, impaired vision or lack of concentration.

A friend of mine recently had an accident because of a wrong decision. He wanted to make a left turn in a rural area of South Jersey. The road he wanted to enter was the main one in that area so he had a stop sign. There was a speeding car on this road coming towards him to his right. To him, it seemed that he had enough time to make the left turn but his judgment was flawed. As he made the left turn, the vehicle coming from the right side crashed into his car. Fortunately, no one was seriously hurt but his insurance company told him that the accident was his fault. My friend was in his eighties and he never should have entered the road at that time. My message to all older drivers is if you are in doubt, do not cross an intersection especially to turn left. Wait until you are positive that it is safe. Statistics show that older drivers are involved in left turn accidents more than any other age group. Do not go if someone behind you beeps the horn at you. If you have an accident, you will be responsible. Your insurance rates will escalate. Insurance companies do not lose money. You will pay for any accident if it is deemed to be your fault.

CHAPTER 8
WHEN TO GIVE UP DRIVING

Senior citizens! How many times have you gone down to the basement for something and when you reached the bottom step you realized that you forgot what you were looking for. Innumerable numbers of older people will readily identify with this frustrating experience. Lack of concentration plus a decreasing attention span are the reasons for this common occurrence. In these laughable incidents no one is hurt except for a possible negative effect on the person's self-esteem.

However, put that same individual behind the wheel of an automobile. Now, lack of attention, concentration and distraction could be disastrous. Today people are living longer and there will be millions of drivers over the age of eighty on the road in the foreseeable future.

Many citizens as a rule drive carefully and have excellent driving records. Inevitably as they get older their motor skills decline. By age forty, nighttime vision starts to deteriorate. At age sixty, drivers need three times the amount of light they needed at age twenty to drive safely at night.

Arthritis can cause stiffness resulting in difficulty looking back over your shoulder. It is also possible to lose feeling in your right foot. Anyone with this condition would have to give up driving since it would be difficult to differentiate between the brake and gas pedal. However, this condition is not very common.

People with diabetes frequently have poor vision. Other conditions which could affect driving are sleep apnea, hearing impairment and medications which may cause confusion and drowsiness.

If you get confused when driving to a familiar destination this is a issue that you should take seriously. There are those who continue driving because they do not wish to lose their independence. This is a dangerous and foolish thing to do. You are endangering yourself and others. If you live long enough, eventually you will have to surrender your driving privileges.

In most cities, transportation is available to all senior citizens for a minimal fee. Included is door-to-door service. Therefore, it is unwise to put your life and others at risk. As people get older they are more susceptible to health disorders such as Alzheimer's Disease, Parkinson's disease and dementia. Others who have suffered heart attacks and not fully recovered are placing themselves in harm's way if they continue to drive.

There are many people who have a valid license but are not capable of driving safely. There are also many people who have had a license for years but seldom drive. Others may have passed an easy driving test and now must learn to drive safely in traffic.

All of those people are a risk to themselves and others, especially those whose driving skills are questionable but do not realize their shortcomings.

Driving a vehicle today is very hazardous. Besides the preceding reasons, there are the aggressive drivers, drunk drivers, sleep deprived drivers and the truck drivers who drive too fast to cover more miles so that they can earn more money.

It is sad but true that there are countless numbers of people who do not have the mental capacity to drive safely. I want to write about a middle-aged neighbor of mine as an example. I stopped at a stop sign in my neighborhood waiting to make a left turn. This particular neighbor was behind me. A car was approaching on my left about two hundred yards away. I very easily made the left turn. To my amazement, she followed me slowly and was struck by the approaching vehicle. When I asked her why she didn't wait, she said that she thought it was safe to follow me.

How do you explain to someone that her reasoning was unsound? A person with her flawed judgment should not be driving. There are countless numbers of people driving today who constantly make wrong decisions.

That is another reason why accidents are inevitable. A driver today must always be alert to possibly avoid accidents with errant or slow-witted drivers. Every day intelligent drivers avoid accidents by skillfully reacting to the mistakes of others.

Vision deterioration if not correctable is enough reason to stop driving. Certain medications can cause drowsiness and affect alertness. Others may cause depression.

There are many seniors who know when to give up driving and know their limitations. If you are starting to have problems driving at night, only drive during the day. Eliminate driving on expressways if you feel insecure driving at high speeds. Do not drive in bad weather. Do not jeopardize your privilege to drive because of stubbornness or false pride. It is better to limit your driving than to lose your license because you would not admit your deficiencies. Be content to be a neighborhood driver and you can do your shopping and drive to your various appointments. By using common sense, you can still be independent and maintain your self-esteem.

One of my favorite quotations is "To thy own self be true." Don't overestimate your driving ability. You may have been a capable driver at one time, but that was then, not now. By not driving you will be able to relax and enjoy life more fully.

If friends and relatives are questioning your driving ability, you must heed their concern for your safety and the well-being of the public. Be examined by a medical doctor and an ophthalmologist. If their examinations confirm the fears of your friends and relatives, you must surrender your license for everyone's safety and peace of mind.

Certainly friends and relatives of the senior drivers in question would be able to recognize the changes in their driving habits. It is the duty of family and/or friends to alert the state if these seniors do not surrender their licenses.

In Pennsylvania, doctors are required by law to report persons whose medical conditions are not acceptable for safe driving.

Actually, it is the responsibility of older drivers to be sensible about their shortcomings. Some of them may not divulge their driving problems to their families or their doctors. A doctor does not evaluate a senior's competence if the senior does not ask for advice.

To surrender your license can be a loss to your pride and self-esteem, but it may be the wisest decision of your life.

Automobile accidents involving seniors happen frequently but are not always reported by the media. Precedence is usually given to the war in Iraq or other news stories. Below are some stories that were reported in the press:

Springfield Township (Delaware County, Pennsylvania) Police said an 88 year old woman from Bryn Mawr, Pennsylvania was driving a 1990 Cavalier station wagon southbound when she collided with a vehicle going westbound on an intersecting road. Paramedics pronounced the woman dead at the scene. The second victim, a 44 year old woman driving a 1995 Subaru Legacy was taken to the hospital. That victim's injuries did not appear to be life-threatening.

Also, two senior citizens were killed in a one-car accident in Doylestown, Pennsylvania. The vehicle crossed the main thoroughfare and veered down a private drive. The car struck a series of trees lining the drive. Witnesses told police that they believed the car was traveling at a high rate of speed.

How many times has a senior driver said after an accident, "I stepped on the gas instead of the brake." This type of accident is inexcusable. Many times the vehicle is out of control and is driven into crowds of people causing many injuries, some fatal.

The drivers in cars in this kind of accident must surrender their licenses for their sake and the public's welfare.

Many years ago people did not live as long as they do today. In those days, a person of sixty was considered old and many drivers stopped driving when they reached the age of sixty-five. Today millions in that age group are driving safely as the life span of people has increased with time. However, as people are living much longer, more will be driving in their eighties and nineties and many will be reluctant to discontinue.

Senior citizens, be honest. If you have doubts or fears about driving, take the time to think about it. Talk it over with your wife, your children, relatives and/or friends. Make the right decision. You will be doing the right thing and everyone will be safer.

A great many drivers are out in the streets that are a menace to others. They lack the skills, judgment and decision-making necessary to be a competent driver. They are dangerous because they are confident and do not realize their shortcomings.

I once taught a middle-aged Russian immigrant who was a very difficult student. He finally passed the driving test on his third attempt. To his befuddled mind, he believed that he was capable of driving everywhere because his state had issued a license to him. He was not lacking in confidence, but that was his own downfall. I advised him to drive in his area until he improved, but he did not take my advice. After he had four inexcusable mishaps, his state revoked his license.

Looking back, I realize that I never should have taught him because he was not driving material or perhaps he lacked "common sense" . From that time on, I refused to teach anyone who I thought would never be capable of being a safe driver. However, I'm sure anyone I advised not to drive would in most cases try another driving school.

Problems Dealing With Seniors

As reported by the AARP Bulletin of November 2006, the number of seniors over sixty-five should double to seventy one million by the year 2030. Approximately 9.5 million drivers would be in their mid-eighties or early nineties. Drivers in this category will no doubt have higher accident rates. In my opinion, lack of concentration will almost always be the reason for accidents by seniors.

About twenty seven states set an age at which drivers must renew their licenses more frequently. At this time only New Hampshire, Illinois and the District of Columbia require road tests for seniors.

There are obstacles facing those states which want to prevent questionable seniors from driving. Protesting seniors would threaten to not vote for those politicians responsible. Retesting would also be an added expense as many more driving examiners would have to be hired.

At this time the problem is very complicated and the solution is not easy. Physical and mental fitness of every senior over seventy should be evaluated by a physician and every senior should be required to get a report by a doctor. This is a procedure which can be accomplished by every state. All those suffering from an onset of dementia or a physical condition which restricts their ability to drive would be taken off the road.

However, there is no way to determine whether a normal senior with no mental or physical deficiencies will lose concentration when behind the wheel. Therefore, the only answer to this dilemma would be to insist that all seniors who repeatedly are involved in preventable accidents be cleared to drive by a physician and be required to take a driving test. Otherwise their licenses should be revoked. This entire situation is very delicate and should be handled with intelligence and empathy. Hopefully, it will be accomplished in the coming years.

Dementia

Dementia is a common problem in the elderly which eventually causes those afflicted to become unsafe drivers. Alzheimer's disease and cerebrovascular disease are 2 common causes of dementia. Many dementia victims are reluctant to surrender their driving privileges even when they commit telltale driving violations. To give up their driving means losing their freedom to be an active member of society. It limits their activities and may make them depressed.

Older drivers cannot hide their shortcomings. Repeated citations such as driving at improper speeds, failing to obey road signs, and lack of concentration will reveal their inability to drive safely. There is no doubt that as we get older, we cannot react safely to different driving situations that occur on the road. Our motor skills, reflexes and coordination decline.

However, not all seniors show signs of dementia. There are many who drive safely and do not get citations for faulty driving.

Concerned physicians play a major role by evaluating seniors in question. Family members alert the physician to demented seniors at risk. Either the doctor will forbid the senior to drive or he will require validation with a road test. If the senior is permitted to drive, he or she should have to take a follow-up test in six months. However, if the questionable driver fails the road test, the license must be voided for everyone's safety including the driver.

The greatest danger to themselves and the public are those showing symptoms of dementia who refuse to stop driving. Only a serious accident will stop them from driving. In many instances most will listen to their friends or relatives, but there will always be those who refuse to relinquish their licenses.

Among them will no doubt be the loners without families who have no one to deter them. This group is the most perilous since they are not being monitored. Drivers with dementia are an ongoing problem which must be addressed.

CHAPTER 9
REVERSE - SHOPPING CENTER - LIMITED ACCESS HIGHWAYS - FREEWAYS

Some people drive for many years and never become proficient when driving in reverse. Unless you have a medical condition which prevents you from turning your head, you should not use the rear mirror as your field of vision will be limited.

If you have difficulty turning your head, be extra watchful using mirrors when parked on the street. Before getting into the car check the area behind you. If any children are playing, caution them to stay away from the back of your car. Go back very slowly and use extreme caution.

To go back straight, place your right hand on the top of the seat next to you and place your left hand near the top of the wheel.

If you want to go back to the right, use both hands to steer to the right and turn your head behind you to the right. To go back to the left, look over your left shoulder and use both hands to turn the wheel. Only use the mirrors if you have difficulty turning your head.

Backing Out of Parking Spaces

Backing out of a parking space in a shopping center has to be one of the riskiest maneuvers for seniors and everyone else.

When going back, try to straighten out until the front of your car passes the rear tires of the cars parked next to you. Back up very slowly so that other vehicles can see you coming out of your space and have time to react if necessary. Now turn the wheel in the direction you want the back of your car to go.

If your exit is on the right, you should now be turning to the left. Be sure to check for pedestrians as well as other cars. Fender benders happen frequently in shopping centers. Although the damage may be minimal, your insurance premium will be increased if you are at fault.

Parking in Shopping Centers

When you are looking for a parking space, keep your foot near the brake and your hand near the horn. If you see a car moving back and the driver not paying attention, honk the horn.

The driving sections of most shopping centers are so constricted that going through them while looking for a parking space can be very frustrating. Of course, they are made this way so that more space is available for parked cars. This makes it risky for the drivers and places pedestrians in danger. A wider area would make it safer for pedestrians and drivers who are trying to park.

Aside from the driving space being wider, every car should be equipped with a beep that goes on every time the driver goes in reverse. Trucks are equipped with this safety feature, but is should be standard on all vehicles. Auto manufacturers should implement this option as standard equipment so that pedestrians would not be in harms way.

Driving in Shopping Centers

It always astonishes me when I see thoughtless drivers going too fast in the midst of pedestrians in a shopping center. The more people walking, the slower you should drive. Under these conditions, five miles per hour or less is necessary. When you are driving alongside the stores, you must stop to let people walk. When people come out of the stores with their merchandise, they usually do not pay attention to moving vehicles. Therefore, it is incumbent for all drivers to yield to pedestrians in this environment. Remember that when you park your car and go shopping you are one of the pedestrians at the mercy of thoughtless drivers.

When a shopping center is very crowded, drivers have to drive around to find a parking space. This creates a hazard for people walking and for all the drivers including those backing out of their spaces as well as those looking for a parking space.

The area used by those looking for a space to park leaves no space for shoppers walking from the stores or going to the stores. When you park, try to go in straight. If your car is not straight or is not centered in the space, back out carefully and go in again. Supermarkets present the greatest dangers because the volume of people who frequent them is much greater. Some people realize this and are very cautious when wheeling their carts. However, there are many who don't drive and who don't pay much attention to the commotion caused by drivers trying to park and those backing out of their spaces. Many people who never drove naively think that all drivers know what they are doing. Unfortunately, this is a fallacy. If all drivers paid attention and always knew what they were doing, the accident rates would be drastically reduced. Therefore, all seniors should stay focused while behind the wheel and when walking to and from a shopping center.

Entering a Freeway or Limited Access Highway

When proceeding into the entrance ramp of a highway, be sure that you are going to the proper entrance. Whether or not you have a yield sign, you must check the traffic on the freeway to get an idea of the traffic scene. Although you may have free access to the extreme right lane, you must realize that when you enter that lane it may be the exit lane for the next exit. If this is the case, when it is safe, move over to the lane on your left.

It is safer and easier if you continue to stay in this lane until you come up towards your exit. You should always be using the next lane to the exit lane until you are a mile or two from your exit. Turn your head quickly to look in the rear and use your right side mirrors a few times before changing to the exit lane. Slow down to the minimum speed (forty or forty-five) when you are about five hundred yards from the exit ramp. Once on the ramp slow down to the speed posted which is usually twenty-five miles per hour or less.

It is possible that an exit will be on your left. When you think that you are approximately two miles from the exit, start trying to move into your extreme left lane. Before changing lanes, put on your left turn signal making sure that no one is on your left. About a half a mile from the exit, put on your left turn signal and reduce your speed to forty miles per hour. As you enter the exit ramp, slow down to the speed specified which should be twenty or twenty-five miles per hour.

You may have to enter a super-highway on the extreme left side. Many times you can enter immediately as the other cars already on the highway are not using the left side. As you drive on, other cars can switch to the extreme left lane. Since speeders usually use all left lanes, it is wise to move over to the lane on the right. Only do so when it is safe.

There are some freeways where you can enter freely, but only for approximately fifty yards. At this point you will encounter a yield sign. Most of the time you will have to stop at the yield sign until it is safe to enter the stream of traffic. Do not be intimidated by a driver behind you who honks his horn at you. You must go only when it is safe to do so. Do not go if you are in doubt. Some aggressive drivers may attempt to force their way into the flowing traffic. When we grow older our perception of approaching speeding vehicles can be deceptive and may have diminished. Only proceed when you positively will not impede or interrupt the flow of traffic of the drivers already on the highway and bring your speed up to or near the speed limit. An accident caused by an impatient or confused driver will have serious consequences.

When older drivers first started to drive some forty, fifty or sixty years ago, the hazards noted did not exist. As time went by many seniors adjusted to the present dangers of the highways, but some did not.

I strongly recommend that as older drivers reach their eighties and beyond they should consider the risks involved and evaluate their ability to cope with the changing traffic scene. If you are starting to feel reluctant and not as sure of yourself as you once were, it would be better to avoid the super highways and find alternate routes. Most of you should be retired so you should not have to live by a time schedule. Avoid stress in your retirement.

CHAPTER 10
USING YOUR VISION CORRECTLY

Questions and Answers

Follow the Dark Streak

Almost every road which has been in use a number of years has a dark streak in the middle of the lane caused by oil droppings

When you are driving on a road with a dark streak in the center of the lane, concentrate on guiding your body over the streak. Scan the road for a distance of one to two blocks depending on your speed. Don't stare. Keep your eyes moving at the traffic scene.

The friend of mine I mentioned previously who had trouble concentrating while driving did much better with his driving while utilizing this tip.

I am including this information to help other seniors with this problem. Following the dark streaks reinforces your steering and your concentration, thus making you a safer driver.

Question: On a narrow winding road, where should I look?

Answer: You should always look in the middle of your lane from curve to curve. Don't look beyond the curve on a winding road and glance at the line on your left to be sure you are close to it.

Question: A school bus is approaching about 100 yards away with the yellow lights flashing. What should I do?

Answer: This means that the bus intends to stop and discharge children. Slow down and stop if the bus stops before you with its upper red lights flashing. You do not proceed until the children are off the street and the bus is moving again.

Question: You are driving on an icy road. You use your brake and go on an icy patch. The rear of the car skids to the right. What do you do?

Answer: Do not jam your brake. Turn the wheel in the direction you want to go which is to the right. When you have straightened out, touch the accelerator lightly to proceed.

Question: What do I do if my car goes through water and affects the brakes?

Answer: Continue to drive slowly and pump the brake pedal lightly until they dry enough so that the car doesn't swerve when you use the brake.

Question: What is a divided highway?

Answer: A divided highway is one with a center or medial barrier built into the highway. Although you are permitted to pass a school bus discharging children if you are on the other side, it is important to be wary of children running across the street. Drivers must be extremely watchful. Children don't understand that cars are permitted to go on a divided highway and they may dart out in front of you. It is your responsibility to be alert and be ready to stop.

Question: You are on your side of a two-lane highway. A car comes towards you partially in your lane. You turn sharply to the right. The right front of your car goes onto the shoulder. What do you do?

Answer: Do not steer back to the lane right away. Ease up on the accelerator and keep a firm grip on the wheel. Pump the brake lightly. When your car slows down go back to your lane carefully.

Question: Is it proper to share a lane with a motorcycle?

Answer: Motorcycles have use of the complete traffic lane. Do not share a lane with one. Do not follow a motorcycle too closely. Stay at least four or five car lengths away.

Question: Is it safe to use high beam lights in fog?

Answer: Never use high beams in foggy weather. It will blind the oncoming drivers. It will also decrease your own ability to see the road. Always use lower beam lights.

Question: Are roads slick at the beginning of a rainfall?

Answer: Yes. As the road dust and oil mix with water the road is very slick.

Question: Why is it dangerous to drive fast during a heavy rainfall?

Answer: Driving too fast can cause hydroplaning so that the tires skim over the ground and you can lose control of your car.

Question: When is it safe to pull in front of a truck?

Answer: It is not safe unless you can see the truck in your rear view mirror. You must never decrease your speed. Trucks need twice as much time to stop than cars do. Unless you are a very skillful driver, it is better to stay away from trucks. A truck driver has three blind spots, right side, left side and rear.

Question: What should you do if you have a flat tire or have a breakdown?

Answer: Drive to the extreme right shoulder of the road making sure that the entire car is on the shoulder. Raise the hood and tie a white cloth to the radio antenna. Use the flashers. Stay off the road.

Question: You are driving on a country road with your wife and three grandchildren. Without warning a rabbit runs in front of your car. If you swerve to the left you will strike another car. If you swerve to the right you will go off the road and probably strike a tree. What should you do?

Answer: You have no choice but to stay straight and hope that the rabbit will not be hurt. You cannot put your family in jeopardy because of the possible demise of a rabbit or any other animal. There are instances like this when the driver swerved and people have been killed.

Question: This question applies mainly for women, but it can also apply to men. You are driving at night on an expressway or a highway. A dark car with a flashing blue light has been following you. He gets along side of you and motions you to pull over. He is not wearing a policeman's uniform, but he points to a badge on his shirt. What should you do?

Answer: If you know you did nothing wrong, do not stop. Get off at the next exit and look for a police car or police station. The man will probably stop following you if you blow your horn non-stop.

Question: What do you do if you are at fault in a traffic accident?

Answer: The worst thing you could possibly do is to drive away from the scene of the accident especially if there are bodily injuries. Many well-known people panic and flee. When they are finally apprehended they are in serious trouble. Do not leave the scene of an accident. Your insurance premium will be increased, but it is the right thing to do and your conscience will be clear. If anyone is injured do not move the person. Call 911 if possible, then exchange information with the other driver. If the accident involves damage to either vehicle, you must report it to the police, the Department of Motor Vehicles and your insurance company. Do not leave the scene of the accident without permission from the police.

Question: If two cars have an accident at an intersection is the driver who had the stop sign solely responsible?

Answer: This is not necessarily so. When an accident occurs at an intersection, both parties may be responsible. When one vehicle goes through a stop sign, the other driver should be able to stop or slow down if he or she is driving defensively. If the driver who does not have a stop sign is speeding, the accident will be partially his/her fault. There are extenuating circumstances in many accidents and all of the facts have to be considered.

Question: Who has the right of way at an unprotected intersection? Consider both streets as equal.

Answer: You must never assume right of way. When both vehicles enter an intersection at the same time the one on the left should yield to the one on the right. If the car on the left arrives at the intersection first and is starting to cross then the car on the right should yield. There are times when you have to yield right of way to an ambulance or a police car with its lights flashing. The bottom line is use common sense in order to prevent an accident.

Question: What do I do if a tire has a "blowout?"

Answer: If a rear tire "blows" out, the back end of the car will swerve. If a front tire "blows" out, the front of the car will swerve. If this happens, do not jam on the brake. Grip the steering wheel and try to keep the car straight. When you have the car under control, apply the brake gently and pull over to the side.

Turned Around Stop Signs

Suppose you come to an intersection that has a stop sign on your right side, but it is turned around. If the sign is on your right side (not across the street), it is your stop sign. Some signs are turned because of loose connections and/or strong winds. If a stop sign is on the right side of your corner, it is for you. If you look diagonally across the intersection you should see the back of a stop sign which should confirm that the turned around sign is for you.

On some streets it could be on your left side of the street because the stop sign on your right side may be hidden. The location of the stop sign is a good indicator for the driver.

Bicycle Riders

More bicycle lanes are now a part of city driving. This development is very perilous for the bicycle rider. In this situation motorists are careless or misinformed. You should not drive in the bicycle lane, especially when making a right turn. When you do turn right and a bicycle lane is on your right, be sure to look in the right side and rear view mirror. Do not turn right if the cyclist is to your right. If you strike a cyclist while turning right, you will be held responsible for a very serious offense.

The Most Irritating Infractions of Drivers

I have compiled a list of annoying practices of some motorists and bicyclists in no special order, but some are worse and more dangerous than others.

1. Drivers who drive partially in your lane.
2. Bicyclists who do not stop for red lights or stop signs.
3. Motorcyclists who deliberately make noise while speeding.
4. Motorists who keep going after their light turns to red, including those with left turn signals.
5. Drivers who drive below the speed limit in the left lane and others who drive at twenty-five miles per hour on a forty-five mile per hour road.
6. Aggressive motorists who exceed the speed limit more than ten miles per hour and tailgate.
7. Drivers who are "horn blowers." These people drive with their horns and not their skills.
8. Drivers who do not know how to make left turns correctly and have been driving for many years.
9. Drivers who back out especially in shopping centers and do not look in the rear first.
10. Drivers who do not slow down on small streets when children are playing.
11. Drivers who habitually do not stop at stop signs.

12. Drivers who double park on the street for a while even though there are legal places to park on the street.

13. Motorists who do not believe in turn signals.

14. Drivers who pull in front of you without enough space.

15. This is a situation which happens frequently if you drive regularly. You are driving on a busy street and the traffic is heavy. Along the way the vehicles slow down and are bumper to bumper. Invariably at some point you will find yourself before an exit from a shopping section. A driver in the shopping area will suddenly decide to pop out of the exit. His move is unexpected since the space is small and if you are not alert his vehicle will strike you or he will hit a vehicle coming from the other direction. This action is especially dangerous because there may not be enough space in the lane of cars coming from the other direction so the risks of an accident are increased.

It is equally as hazardous when a driver coming towards you decides to suddenly turn in front of you to enter the shopping section. These incidents happen frequently by thoughtless drivers so everyone should be aware of this danger.

I know there are many more, but I have listed those which I thought were most important.

All seniors should refrain from committing the preceding errors noted above. Some of these mistakes could kill you or others in your vehicle. A driver must be alert and take the necessary action against drivers who break the traffic rules. It is not enough today for a motorist to obey all the traffic rules, but he or she must be able to react properly to the infractions of other drivers or else bear the consequences.

CHAPTER 11
VITAL RULES FOR SENIORS
AND EVERYONE ELSE

In March 2004, it was estimated that drivers over sixty-five were increasing three times as fast as all other age groups. As this trend continues, more scrutiny will be placed on the driving habits of our aging population. Accordingly, senior drivers should be aware of this imminent crisis. It is likely that all senior drivers over a specified age will be asked to undergo a re-examination. Whether it will be a physical or driving test is uncertain. My guess is that many will have to take a driving examination and those in good shape and free of accidents or violations will be told to visit the State Police for an eye test. It is possible that all drivers over eighty years of age will have to take a driving test. When and if this comes to pass, seniors should not panic. The wise ones will drive carefully and avoid traffic violations.

The following is a short summary of rules for seniors to abide by.

Don't tailgate and don't slow down when someone is tailgating you. You never know what kind of person is behind you. He may be drunk or on drugs. Slowing down could infuriate him further especially if he has no space to pass you. If possible pull over to the side.

Don't give anyone the "finger" when driving. You are too old for that nonsense and too old to protect yourself from an enraged driver younger and stronger than you.

Left turns - Watch out for drivers facing you who turn left as soon as the light turns to green or turn left after the light turns red. Infractions of left turns are constant. Improper left turns cause accidents everyday and everywhere. Don't add your name to the multitudes of drivers who commit these violations.

Don't assume right of way even if you have a green light or no stop sign. Protect yourself against aggressive drivers, drunkards and those on drugs. A simple procedure like placing your foot over the brake pedal for a second at intersections when you have a green light can prevent an accident. This action exemplifies defensive driving.

If you are going to make a turn at an intersection, put on your turn signal in advance. Try to remember this particularly when you are stopping for a red light at a busy intersection. There are some drivers who do not use signals and there are those who habitually put on the turn signal after they have stopped. The motorists behind those thoughtless drivers have every right to be annoyed. This is another infraction which seniors should try to avoid so as not to ruin their driving reputations.

It will make your driving safer and easier if you do not drive a large vehicle. . These cars require more skill in driving and parking. You are not the same driver you were thirty years ago. Be smart. A car the size of a Toyota Corolla or a similar vehicle would be best suited for older people.

Do not plan to drive if there is a threat of snow. Driving while the snow is falling is especially hazardous. Not only do you have to cope with the slippery surface of the road, but your vision will be hampered. There are times when it is difficult to keep the windshield clean while snow is falling. Do not place yourself in a precarious environment needlessly.

If you ever find yourself wanting to shut your eyes momentarily, pull off the road and rest your eyes. It is better to be late than cause an accident. Traffic today is too complex. It needs your full attention. Senior drivers need eight hours of sleep in spite of misinformation to the contrary. If you are sleepy because of a poor night's sleep, you should not drive.

Do not allow drivers behind you to affect your driving. As a driver for many years, I can sympathize with drivers affected by those driving behind them. If you are driving correctly, you should be glancing in the rear view mirror every five or ten seconds. No doubt you have noticed a driver behind you trying to push you to go faster. It is an ongoing occurrence. It can be very annoying and aggravating. You must continue to drive at the specified speed limit and not go faster to accommodate the other driver. It is very important to not let your driving be affected. This type of driver is on every road and these situations will always exist.

Never stop suddenly unless it is to avoid hitting another car or person. If you are alert, you can prevent jamming your brake by driving defensively. That is another reason why you should always be aware of the traffic behind you. If you know what's behind you, you will know what to do. If you are driving on a narrow street with parked cars on both sides, be aware of children. Beep your horn and keep your foot near the brake.

When you are the designated driver and letting passengers out of your car, put the lever into Park "P" and put on the emergency brake. Do not allow your passengers to move until you do this. Also, when they are in the car while you are driving, insist that everyone use a seatbelt.

Always drive with patience. If people drove with more patience, accidents would be reduced tremendously. The problem with today's world is that too many people are in a hurry. Perhaps they are late for their job or late for an appointment. Others habitually drive too fast. Lack of patience could be the greatest reason for traffic accidents.

Never forget to check traffic behind you when first starting to drive from a parked position. A young lady who I taught to drive had just purchased her first new car. She was so excited the first time she drove it that she neglected to check the rear. The inevitable happened. Her car was struck by a car from the rear. If the motorist behind her was more observant and cautious, an accident could have been avoided. An alert driver should be observant of anyone sitting in a parked car who possibly could be getting ready to pull out in front of them.

There is no doubt that a senior driver will be more likely to be distracted or lose concentration when driving alone in the car. Therefore, in this situation he or she should be especially alert and pay strict attention to the traffic conditions. There recently have been instances of seniors driving into houses, buildings and a woman who backed into a crowd of people. In every accident, the senior driver was alone in the car.

When you are driving on any multi-lane highway, always keep to the right. Many people are killed or maimed when they're struck by an oncoming vehicle which has strayed over the centerline. Don't take unnecessary risks. There are drunks, people on drugs and drowsy drivers on the road.

Changing Lights

One of the most precarious decisions a driver has to make is whether to stop or go at a changing light. This situation arises almost every time you get behind the wheel.

To my observation, many drivers go through yellow lights carelessly. Slow down at an intersection with a "stale" green light so that you can stop safely if the light changes to yellow, rather than having to accelerate through a yellow light that changes to red while you are still in the middle of the intersection. If you do this , you risk getting a ticket.

Presently, there is no viable solution to this vexing problem. Drivers have a mind-set to drive through changing lights and unless traffic lights were to be more definitive, this situation will exist.

Suppose you are a driver who wants to obey the traffic rules. Therefore, when you are in doubt about going through a changing signal, you stop. However, the motorist behind you does not expect you to stop so he has to jam his brake or he will crash into your vehicle. Many times when I am behind the wheel, I am afraid to stop at a changing light because a car is close behind me. Therefore, I must make a quick decision. Usually I will not stop and the driver behind me illegally follows me.

This is a pervasive situation which continues unabated. Every driver must make the decision to stop or go. If you are in heavy traffic, it is safer to drive through changing lights to avoid being struck from behind. However, you should not drive through stale yellow lights to accommodate the driver behind you. This action is not a panacea for changing lights, but driving in today's traffic is fraught with peril for all drivers and passengers.

CHAPTER 12
THE DRIVING TEST

When a teenager is preparing for a driving test, he or she can't wait. The time goes by too slowly. They look forward with impatience to the day when they get behind the wheel and drive with their peers looking on with envy.

However, when seniors are preparing for the driving test, their attitude is one of apprehension and fear. Exuberance and confidence diminishes in most people as the years go by.

Unfortunately, as people are living longer, many will be faced with the unpleasant prospect of submitting to a driving re-examination. The traffic conditions in the United States (also worldwide) are getting more complex. Drivers are continuing to drive in their seventies and eighties. As they age, their skills will certainly deteriorate causing them to be involved in accidents caused by their lack of concentration or short attention span.

Many of them will choose to forfeit their license because of lack of confidence and an unwillingness to endure the stress and pain involved in a re-examination. It is for those who will not surrender their independence and who need their license desperately that I am sharing my knowledge and experience to help them retain their driving privileges. If you haven't lost your skill and are in fairly good health (including eyesight), do not panic. If you prepare yourself thoroughly, you will be successful.

For those who are overly confident, I have witnessed skillful teenagers who failed their driving test because of over confidence as exemplified by the teenager who thought he could show how great he was by driving with one hand on the wheel.

Do not be too proud to go to a good driving school. If you take the re-examination in the driving school's car, the examiner will be more relaxed because of the double brake. Driving examiners are like you and I. Some of them get nervous when giving exams. Many an examiner has commented to me and said, "Your applicant gave me a good ride."

Another reason to go to a driving school is that your instructor will show you the most asked questions in the driving manual. To pass the test you must answer the questions correctly as well as pass the driving portion of the test.

In Philadelphia, Pennsylvania, the State Police have nothing to do with driving examinations. The Pennsylvania Department of Transportation supervises all driving tests. Civilians called "driving examiners" conduct all driving tests.

If you have committed a driving violation, you may be requested to take a re-examination or forfeit your license.

In Pennsylvania you must successfully answer computerized questions taken from the driving manual. You cannot take the driving test until you pass the written part of the exam. Therefore, do not go for the questions before you have studied the driver's manual.

It is likely that many cities in different states also employ civilians to conduct driving tests. If you are summoned to take a re-examination, it would be wise to familiarize yourself with your state requirements.

You can fail the test for the following reasons:

1. Failing to use proper signals.
2. Driving too slowly.
3. Driving too fast.
4. Not coming to a complete stop at the stop signs.
5. Not keeping both hands on the wheel.
6. Not turning hand-over-hand.
7. Not knowing the answers to questions asked.
8. Not following the directions of the examiner.
9. Not following the course correctly.
10. Not releasing the emergency brake before starting out.

Many cities and towns do not have separate driving courses. If you are taking a re-examination you may take the test on the street or a combination of a driving course and traffic on the city streets. Usually the applicant is taken on a particular route in traffic. If this would apply to you, my suggestion would be to follow a person taking the test or at the very least know the complete route. The route may not always be the same, but it will be somewhat similar. If you take the test on the street, be sure you abide by the speed limit. Do not drive too slowly. Put on your signals in advance, not at the intersection, if possible. Yield to pedestrians. For left turns at a traffic light, go out halfway on the green light and proceed when you do not interfere with oncoming traffic. At the beginning of the test, put on a left signal and look in the rear if you are pulling out from a parked position on the right. At every stop sign come to a complete stop and do not move for at least three seconds. If you stop at a four-way stop sign, do not go if a car is on your right unless you arrive at the stop sign at least ten seconds before the other car.

At the beginning of the test, your motor should be turned off, the emergency brake must be on and in an automatic car, the lever should be in"Park." You may be asked to put on the signals and lights before starting.

Unfortunately, human nature plays a part in the decisions of the driving examiners. A pretty woman or cute teenager will almost always get preferential treatment from a male examiner. Some examiners are lenient and others are strict. Some are pleasant and some are nasty. Authority also affects some driving examiners especially those who previously held menial jobs before they became driving examiners.

It is important for the applicant not to irritate the examiner. If he or she seems pompous or not inclined to talk, don't initiate conversation. Don't ever do what a young lady did when she told the examiner to put on his seatbelt. He was so annoyed that he failed her when she committed a very minor mistake.

At the beginning of the test try to form a judgment of the examiner. If he or she is friendly, it is alright to converse but don't overdo it. Many examiners want to maintain an established ratio of failures so if they are having a bad day, they will help you pass. However, some examiners have bad reputations and don't care. But a surly demeanor by the examiner will almost surely affect the applicant's driving. If you are unfortunate enough to get such an examiner, remember you can come back and get another chance to retain your license.

For those of you who are too fearful to undertake a re-examination, follow my instructions and you will be successful. If your family and friends tell you that you have the necessary skill to drive, go for it. You have nothing to lose and everything to gain; namely your independence and self-esteem.

Be Prepared

In all my experience in the driving training field, the most important rule for people taking the driving test was that they be thoroughly prepared. Anyone taking a driving test is nervous. Teenagers, can surmount nervousness better than seniors. However, the more prepared you are the easier it is to master nervousness. When you can automatically drive well without thinking about it, you are more apt to succeed.

Many people, especially teenagers, take the exam before they are ready. Nervousness takes over and mistakes are made. As a rule, seniors are prone to be more apprehensive than younger people. My advice to seniors taking the test for the first time or taking a re-exam is that he or she not attempt it until they are completely familiar with every part of the exam. When they think they are ready, they should practice more until they can do it all automatically.

CHAPTER 13
WHAT GRANDPARENTS
SHOULD KNOW

Grandparents adore their grandchildren. It is extremely important to know how to keep grandchildren safe when they travel in an automobile. There are laws concerning traveling with children in automobiles which may vary from state to state. It is important to check the state laws of your particular state regarding child restraints. Also, each car seat has instructions which are specific to that car seat. Read them carefully and always register the car seat with the manufacturer to ensure that you will be made aware of any recalls or problems with the seat. Below are some of the most important general rules which apply to seatbelts and restraint systems:

1. Infants and babies under twenty pounds require infant car seats. They should be properly secured in a child restraint system in the back seat of the car facing the rear. Older

children require front facing car seats or booster seats. Infant car seats and front facing car seats use what is known as a five (5) point harness system. Older children, usually over forty (40) pounds, and up to approximately seventy-five (75) pounds require booster seats. Booster seats are front facing car seats which utilize the car's shoulder harness seat belts. In addition to a child's weight, the child's height is also a factor in determining the appropriate restraint system

2. The child should never be allowed to lean against the door or be near the door because of the danger of inflating side airbags or curtain shield airbags.

3. Do not allow a child sitting in the front to be on the edge of the seat. If the front airbags inflate, the child would be seriously or fatally injured. Move the seat back as far as possible.

4. Be sure that all doors are closed and locked.

5. If a child is too large for a restraint system, the child should sit in the rear in a seatbelt.

6. Follow instructions in the seat's manual for securing the child restraint seat.

7. As a general rule, children are safer when secured in the rear.

8. Never place a baby in the front seat. Remember that an airbag can be activated by sudden stops as well as accidents.

9. Never hold a small child on your lap whether sitting in the front seat or rear seat.

10. The child should be properly secured in the seat, snug, but not too tight to restrict the child's breathing.

11. Taking the necessary precautions for your grandchildren is a positive affirmation of your love for them.

Taking Care of Your Vehicle

Taking care of your vehicle is a must for your safety and the safety of others. It helps to maintain a good relationship with a mechanic in the service station you go to so he will take a personal interest in your car. In our old age, we may neglect the care and procedures required to keep a car running smoothly so the list below should be followed.

Always check the tires and see that they are properly inflated. Incorrect tire pressure can reduce your mileage. Always have your tires checked and rotated when needed. Don't forget to check your spare tire. It is best to check your tires before driving, especially when your tires are old. Tires that are not inflated properly will affect the steering. A reliable mechanic is your best option. Don't ever try to change a flat. You are too old for that. Join an auto club for your peace of mind.

Fluids to Watch

1. Check your engine oil after three thousand miles or after three or four months. If you continue to use your car without changing the oil, the engine may be severely damaged. Your service station should also replace the oil filter.
2. The automatic transmission fluid normally should be replaced after twenty-five or thirty thousand miles. Your service station should flush the fluid completely and replace it with fresh fluid. This will replace all the fluid in the transmission.
3. Brake fluid should be changed every two years unless you detect a leak sooner. If so, have your mechanic look at it.

4. If your steering wheel is hard to turn, have your power steering fluid checked.

5. The air filter should be changed once or twice a year.

6. Every few months, have your mechanic look at your hoses or belts for wear. Always examine them with the motor turned off.

7. Periodically check the blades of your windshield wipers. Replace the blades if they are not cleaning the windshield effectively.

8. Check your heater, defroster and fan. Use the air conditioner sometimes in the winter to ensure that it is working efficiently.

9. Anti-freeze should be checked yearly and usually replaced after two or sometimes three years to prevent freezing.

10. After approximately thirty thousand miles, the shocks and struts may have to be replaced. Some of the signals are as follows:

   a. Your car may bounce after colliding with an object or a bump in the road.

   b. Your tires are not wearing evenly.

   c. Steering is not normal.

   d. You detect leakage.

   e. Your car does not stay on course when turning corners.

   These are the times to have your struts or shocks inspected by your service station. If would be foolish and dangerous to procrastinate.

11. Do not use cruise control on icy or slick roads. The car may veer out of control.

12. Bear in mind that driving at dawn or dusk is not the best time to drive as visibility is poor.

13. Try to observe traffic on city streets by glancing up and down for one half block to a full block (about 500 feet).

14. Do not drive your car with dirty windows. Keep the rear windows clean as well as the windshield.

15. Your service station should check the different lights - headlights, taillights, signals, hazard lights, *etc.*

16. After washing your car, do not let it air dry. It could damage the paint by causing streaks and blemishes.

There are many other parts of a car to be checked. However, you are not a mechanic so let your service station take care of it.

Donating Your Car

If you wish to donate your car to a worthwhile charity, you should know the laws regarding tax deductions. The present law now will allow you to deduct only the amount the charity will receive when selling your vehicle no matter if your car is worth more. So if your car is worth three thousand dollars and the charity sells it for only two thousand dollars, you may only deduct two thousand dollars from your income tax. However, it is best to consult with your accountant to be sure before you surrender your vehicle. He should be aware of the IRS guidelines.

How Grandparents Help

If grandparents desire to help their children by occasionally taking care of the grandchildren, it is a necessity that they know how to drive safely. When couples marry at an early age, they find themselves grandparents in their late forties or early fifties. Under these circumstances, the parents probably will be working in order to fill the needs of their young family. Grandparents may be asked to babysit, take their grandchildren to school, or pick them up after school. It would not be unusual for grandparents to take care of the young children while their parents go on vacation.

It would be a tremendous hardship to the parents if the grandparents do not drive. However, those in their fifties or sixties should be better drivers than those in their seventies and eighties. In those situations, the parents should evaluate the driving capability of the grandparents. Children are too precious to place them in jeopardy.

Grandfathers should not be too vain to not allow their wives to drive the children if they are the better drivers.

People in their sixties have better driving records than teenagers. Grandparents in their eighties should be certain that they are capable drivers so that they can transport their grandchildren safely. Mom-moms and pop-pops adore their grandchildren and the feelings are mutual.

Cell Phones

It has been established that using cell phones while driving was distracting and responsible for many accidents. The introduction of hands-free cell phones was believed to have solved the indiscriminate use of cell phones. However, a new study by the University of California found that talking on the phone while driving was a distraction, hands-free or not. Hands-free was an improvement but still was a hazard on the highways. Texting while driving is particularly dangerous.

A few states have laws that require drivers to use hands-free cell phones. Cell phones are not the only distraction for drivers on the roads. Distracted driving of any kind should be avoided-this includes playing with the radio, putting on makeup, looking for something on the seat or floor of the car, eating a sandwich, adjusting a child's seat, or anything else that will take one's attention away from driving safely. If any of these activities is necessary, pull the car over and stop before proceeding. Older people should not be using cell phones of any kind while driving. If your phone beeps, your attention to the road is diverted. In the once popular song, "Yesterday," is a line which goes like this, "I am not the man I used to be." Could there be a more truthful aphorism than that? The bottom line is that when you are behind the wheel don't let your mind wander. Focus on the road.

Senior Pedestrians

It is a known fact that regular walking will prolong your life. Senior men and women should walk to maintain good health and retard aging. You don't need expensive equipment and you don't have to join a gym. If you are over eighty and motivated enough you will get out and walk at least twenty minutes a day. If you are under sixty-five, walk a half hour to an hour. You should walk five days each week. In bad weather, try walking in your house. It is important not to sit around and watch television. If you are one of those couch potatoes, break the habit. Most of the programs on television are not even worth watching. Your health is more important than watching soap operas.

I knew a man ninety years old who walked everyday. Unfortunately, as he was walking and not concentrating, he stepped out to his left and a speeding car struck him and fatally injured him. The walker committed an error which is also deadly for drivers. He went out of his lane without looking in the rear and it cost him his life.

To be safe when walking, do not walk in the street with traffic behind you. If you must walk, especially in a rural section without pavements, walk facing traffic. The same rule does not apply to bicycle riders. They should always go with traffic. Many bicycle riders are not aware of this and they ride against the traffic. This is especially true of young people. If you have grandchildren with bicycles, enlighten them so that they will not endanger their lives.

A Preventable Accident

This is an important message to all seniors and all other drivers. When you are driving, particularly on a country road, do you pass joggers or walkers without warning them of your approach?

How many people have to be killed or maimed by thoughtless drivers? The jogger or walker who darts in front of the vehicle will usually pay with his life for his carelessness. Therefore, it is the thoughtless driver whose conscience must bear the brunt of the misfortune since the driver is rarely injured.

The driver must never assume that the jogger on his side will not suddenly cross over in front of him. Many joggers or walkers are listening intently to music (with earplugs) and are oblivious to the approach of your vehicle.

Just recently in May 2007, a teenager girl was jogging (not facing traffic) on a country road listening to her favorite music with ear plugs. Without thinking she crossed over into the path of a vehicle driven by another teenager from the same school. Unfortunately, the jogger was killed. Because of this tragedy, the lives of two families will be forever affected and the driver will suffer the rest of her life for destroying another human life. The teenage driver was guilty of doing what many others would have done. A simple toot of her horn would have prevented this calamity. She may also have been listening to her radio and not paying attention to the road as well.

What happened that day is inexcusable. Vehicle accidents are happening every day, but this is one type of accident that should never happen.

Seniors should be aware of this sort of catastrophe which calls for complete concentration. The solution to those preventable accidents is ironically simple. A driver must never assume that a walker or jogger moving on their side will not cross in front of them. They must not day dream and they must stay focused. Before passing the pedestrian, the driver must tap the horn to warn the jogger and slow down.

These unfortunate tragedies can also be prevented if the jogger or walker faces traffic on the shoulder or side of the road. A pedestrian will rarely be struck by a vehicle if he or she is facing oncoming traffic.If the drivers and pedestrians observed these simple rules, countless numbers of lives would be saved.

Driving a Stick Shift

It is strongly recommended that seniors drive automobiles with automatic transmissions. Although no doubt there are many seniors driving stick shift cars, traffic today has become much more complicated compared to forty or fifty years ago. With a stick shift car, you have to use the clutch and shift gears simultaneously as well as steer at the same time. You may not realize that you are not as skilled as you once were. Your reaction time, attention span and coordination have diminished. If you are still driving a manual transmission vehicle, do yourself a favor and switch to an automatic.

CHAPTER 14
CONCLUSION

Get behind the wheel of your car and drive in any city or populated area. If you drive for at least twenty minutes and you have not observed a traffic infraction, it would be most unusual. If you continue to drive, this is most likely what you will see- drivers not stopping when the green signal changes to red, drivers trying to pass with insufficient space, drivers going well over the speed limit and many not stopping at stop signs. Most older drivers are not speeders, but their deficiencies are just as dangerous.

Accidents could be reduced drastically if traffic regulations were enforced more vigorously. This cannot be accomplished unless more police are hired to enforce the rules. This would involve an outlay of more money which seems unlikely considering other civic problems which mistakenly appear to be more urgent. To expect every driver to obey the traffic rules is wishful thinking.

In March 2005, after much publicity, the City of Philadelphia placed photo cameras at a very busy intersection on the Roosevelt

Boulevard. In its first week of operation, 1,569 drivers received citations for driving through red lights. By the end of the month, 5,169 drivers were photographed passing through on the red light. These violations are hard to explain since every driver in the area knew about the location of these cameras. This illustrates the mind-set of many drivers. They habitually go through red lights and evidently bad habits do not die easily. Perhaps after they pay the one hundred dollar fine they will be more aware of the consequences, but they will continue to drive through red lights at other intersections which do not have cameras.

Road Rage

There is no logical reason for a motorist to kill another motorist over a traffic controversy, but it happens frequently. Usually it begins when an aggressive driver passes too close to another motorist or suddenly cuts in front of him.

A familiar pattern follows. The offended one starts to chase the aggressive driver. When the aggressive one stops, the other one gets out of his car, the tempers flare and violence erupts.

It's possible that one of them, or even both of them, are drunk or on drugs and may even have a gun. In this dangerous condition these men do not hesitate to kill. They fancy themselves to be kings of the road. When their driving space is infringed upon they take it as a personal affront.

I have witnessed a road rage incident which had to be to seen to be believed. Two cars were racing side by side while the passenger in one car was exchanging blows with the driver of the other car. This continued for a few minutes until one driver pulled away.

There are psychotic people driving who are placing the public in jeopardy. Unfortunately, they continue to drive until they cause injuries or fatalities.

Recently in Pennsylvania a drunken driver struck a sixty-one year old man's vehicle. Unfortunately, the older man got out of his car and confronted the aggressor who pulled out a gun and killed him. The victim was both a father and a grandfather who was very much loved by his family. These tragedies happen often and will continue to happen. The only way they can be averted is to never confront or incite the other person. Walk away to live another day.

Drunk Drivers

Approximately forty percent of fatalities on the road are caused by drunk drivers. Although the blood alcohol level has been lowered in many States, the solution to this alarming problem is too complex. People will continue to drink and drive until they are punished more severely.

Alcoholics who get citations for drunken driving are usually habitual offenders. Taking away their drivers licenses does not stop them from driving. The habitual offender should serve time in prison. The number of lives that have been shattered and will be shattered is incalculable. The sorrow and tragedies caused by drunken drivers are worldwide.

It is an inescapable fact that as time goes by the ranks of older drivers will grow. It follows that more of them will be involved in accidents caused by lack of concentration. Of course, there is no excuse for this type of accident, but they will surely happen. The public and media could demand re-exams.

However, there should also be stricter rules for teenagers and young people in their early twenties to abstain from alcoholic drinks and speeding. How many times do young people have to die needlessly because of their reckless driving behind the wheel? The problem of young people being killed on the road is more urgent and happens more frequently than accidents caused by senior drivers.

Statistics show that older drivers over seventy-five and into their eighties are more prone to having accidents. Many of them are caused by lack of concentration or drowsiness resulting from medications or lack of sleep.

Many in this group realize their limitations and will voluntarily limit their driving. However, there will always be those who will overestimate their driving ability.

Always remember just before you get behind the wheel to tell yourself that you are going to focus completely on the road ahead and not let yourself be distracted by anything on the side. Do not risk hurting others and yourself or destroying property. Protect your driver's license with responsibility and vigilance.

It doesn't matter how skillful a driver you once were or still think you are. Lack of concentration has to be the greatest shortcoming of older drivers. You cannot turn back the clock, but you can make an effort to concentrate all of the time you are driving.

Look Ahead

Your eyes should be constantly scanning the traffic scene ahead of you, behind you and along side of you. Take quick glances. Never stare.

YOUR EYES AND BRAIN WORK TOGETHER. YOUR BRAIN TELLS YOU WHAT TO DO AFTER GETTING THE MESSAGE FROM YOUR EYES. IF YOUR EYES LOOK IN THE WRONG PLACE, YOUR BRAIN WILL RECEIVE THE WRONG MESSAGE FROM YOUR EYES. CONSEQUENTLY, YOU COULD STEER INCORRECTLY OR BRAKE AT THE WRONG TIME AND CAUSE AN ACCIDENT.

Since people are living longer, the ranks of older drivers will be growing steadily. As they enter their eighties, their driving ability and judgment will surely diminish.

Currently about ten percent of the nation's drivers are over sixty-five. By the year 2030, an estimated one in five Americans will be sixty-five or older, with those aged eighty and up to exceed ten million.

Therefore, it is incumbent for them to maintain safe driving habits or many states will impose re-examinations or revoke their licenses.

Being a senior citizen myself, I know how easy it is to lose my concentration. Be sure to see all stop signs and red lights. If you are driving to a new place, be sure you know exactly how to get there. Only drive at night if your ophthalmologist gives you permission. When driving with other people, pay attention to the traffic and don't join in the conversation. Stay within the speed limit and, I repeat, <u>stay focused</u>!

Years ago people in their seventies were considered fortunate to be alive let alone able to drive a vehicle. Today many in their seventies and eighties are productive, vigorous citizens who are contributing their skills to society. However, when reaching their late eighties and early nineties, the passage of time takes its toll.

As people age they also fall when walking because of frailty, lack of concentration and difficulty maintaining their balance. Many of the frail ones will tend to die sooner or spend the rest of their lives in a wheel chair.

People will continue to live longer and continue to drive. Those who drive with complete concentration will survive, but many will have to surrender their driving privilege because of their accidents caused by lack of concentration, attention span, *etc.*

Finally, if your family or friends advise you to stop driving, you probably should. Don't end your driving career with a serious or fatal accident.

After driving almost a lifetime, many older drivers may not realize how much their driving skills have diminished. When we get older, our faculties have deteriorated. There are no exceptions. You can't think as quickly, your reaction time is slower and your hearing and vision are not as sharp. I want to make this clear - - the purpose of this book is not to discourage seniors from driving, but to warn them about future laws which will insist that they be re-examined. Frankly, I do not know if all seniors after a certain age will be called for re-exams or only those who commit inexcusable driving infractions. However, you can be sure that as the number of older drivers escalates, all of them or a percentage of them will be summoned for re-examinations. Various states have different laws now regarding older people retaking the road test. As times goes by more and more states will enact laws for re-exams as well.

The truth is that seniors in their sixties have better driving records than most age groups. As a rule, they do not tailgate and do not speed. As people go into their seventies and eighties, different problems arise. Most of these can be rectified with intelligent solutions. There are treatments for impaired vision or hearing problems. Larger mirrors would be beneficial to combat imperfect vision and wearing yellow tinted sunglasses would help daytime glare.

Every driver must evaluate himself or herself and act accordingly. As you get older, limit your driving. Protect your privilege to drive by making intelligent decisions. Being older does not lessen your need to drive. Older people need car transportation as well as anyone else.

It must be noted that drivers over sixty-five have the second highest fatality record of all age groups. One reason being is that older people do not recover from serious injuries as well as younger people.

It is my belief that lack of concentration is the single most destructive factor affecting the driving of older people. This weakness causes more mishaps and serious accidents now and it will become progressively worse unless seniors make a concerted effort to focus one hundred percent when out on the road.

Publications by AARP and AAA on the subject of senior drivers do not emphasize lack of concentration enough. However, as someone who has been in the driver-training field for thirty-six years, I see the situation differently. Lack of concentration should be at the top of the list for the cause of seniors' accidents.

As time goes by and millions of octogenarians continue to drive, lack of concentration will prove to be the greatest detriment to them. Many will be on the road suffering from dementia and other diseases that could affect their ability to drive safely. Even healthy drivers in their late eighties and early nineties will be a concern because of their advanced age.

I strongly recommend that as older drivers reach their eighties and beyond, they should consider the risks involved and evaluate their ability to cope with the changing traffic scene. If you are starting to feel reluctant and not as sure of yourself as you once were, it would be better to avoid the super highways and find alternative routes. Most of you should be retired so you should not have to live by a time schedule. Avoid stress in your retirement.

Therefore, senior drivers must make a conscious effort to be alert and drive a little slower. If you are not sure of nighttime driving, don't venture into strange areas. Each person should know his or her limitations. As people get older into their late eighties, they should restrict their driving to familiar areas at night.

It is the responsibility of these older drivers to maintain safe driving habits for their own survival. Their fate is in their hands.

It is obvious that the great hazard facing the older driver now and in the future years is to overcome inclinations towards distractions, daydreaming and lack of concentration.

This perilous situation will not be easy to overcome, but it can be ameliorated by safety minded, knowledgeable senior drivers.

To all senior drivers, drive safely and good luck